Hiking Colorado's Front Range

Second Edition

Bob D'Antonio

FALCONGUIDES

GUILFORD, CONNECTICUT
HELENA, MONTANA
AN IMPRINT OF GLOBE PEQUOT PRESS

To buy books in quantity for corporate use
or incentives, call **(800) 962-0973**
or e-mail **premiums@GlobePequot.com.**

FALCONGUIDES®

FalconGuides is an imprint of Globe Pequot Press.
Falcon, FalconGuides, and Outfit Your Mind are registered trademarks of Morris Book Publishing, LLC.

TOPO! Explorer software and SuperQuad source maps courtesy of National Geographic Maps. For information about TOPO! Explorer, TOPO!, and Nat Geo Maps products, go to www.topo.com or www.natgeomaps.com.

Project editor: David Legere
Layout: Sue Murray
Interior photos by Bob D'Antonio unless otherwise credited

Maps created by Trailhead Graphics Inc. © Morris Book Publishing, LLC

Library of Congress Cataloging-in-Publication Data is available on file.

ISBN 978-0-7627-7085-4

Printed in the United States of America

10 9 8 7 6 5 4 3 2

Contents

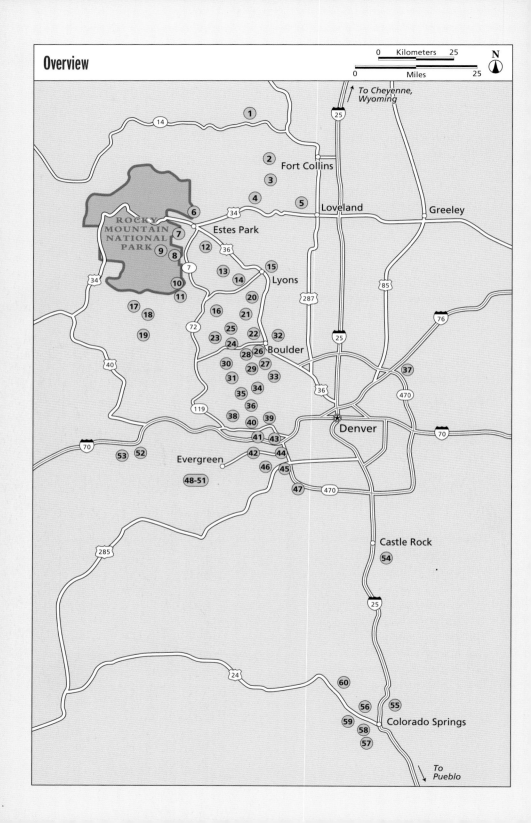

0   Kilometers   25

0   Miles   25

N

To Cheyenne, Wyoming

Fort Collins

Loveland

Greeley

ROCKY MOUNTAIN NATIONAL PARK

Estes Park

Lyons

Boulder

Denver

Evergreen

Castle Rock

Colorado Springs

To Pueblo

Introduction

The Front Range of Colorado is an area that roughly extends from Fort Collins in the north to Pueblo in the south. This book explains in detail sixty hikes from Fort Collins to Colorado Springs. It is a spectacular area of low-lying plains, rounded foothills, towering mountain peaks, wide open meadows, free-flowing rivers and streams, beautiful alpine lakes, glaciers, narrow gulches, tall rock walls, and views that extend in all directions. It is also an area of tremendous vertical relief: From the mile-high city of Denver you can travel west and in a mere 35 miles gain over 8,000 feet in altitude.

At the heart of this great vertical topography are the southern Rocky Mountains and the Continental Divide. Colorado has the highest mountains in the Rocky Mountains and claims fifty-four summits over 14,000 feet high. The Continental Divide runs in a north-to-south direction near the center of the state and controls the flow of water from rivers and streams on both sides: West of the divide water flows to the Gulf of California; on the east side water flows into the Gulf of Mexico.

Between the plains and the high mountains are the foothills, a place of mixed forests, wide open meadows filled with cacti, yuccas, wildflowers, various shrubs, pinyon, junipers, ponderosas, aspens, tall cottonwoods, Douglas firs, and spruce trees. It is a place myriad animals call home. Mountain lions, elk, white-tailed deer, mule deer, prairie dogs, Abert's squirrels, high flying hawks, bald and golden eagles, prairie falcons, Canada geese, and other migratory birds can be found in this very diverse area. More than 960 species of animals call the open lands of the Front Range home. You can walk through most open areas and spot or hear one or many of these animals. Coyotes sing as they hunt at night; elk bugle in the fall looking for mates; bighorn sheep roam the high country and climb steep rock walls with sure-footed moves that would make any climber envious. Hawks and eagles fill the sky looking for food and cruising on thermals, diving and looking as though they don't have a care in the world.

There are five different life zones in the Front Range of Colorado. The Upper Sonoran is an area of high desert, filled with stunted pinyon, small ponderosas, juniper trees, cacti, yuccas, and prairie grasses. It ranges from 4,000 to 6,000 feet above sea level. Next is the Transition Zone, an area that ranges from 6,000 to 8,000 feet above sea level. Tall ponderosas, Douglas firs, Gambel and mahogany oaks, various wildflowers, and the occasional lodgepole pine are found here. Above the Transition Zone is the Canadian Zone, an area that extends roughly from above 8,000 feet to nearly 10,000 feet in altitude. This zone is much cooler than the lower elevations and sees more precipitation. Common trees include aspens, Engelmann spruce, and lodgepole pines. Wildflowers thrive in this zone, as do many animal species.

Next is the Hudsonian Zone, an area rising from 10,000 feet to above timberline, roughly around 11,000 feet above sea level. This zone is home to hardy

Looking west from Pawnee Pass, Indian Peaks Wilderness

species of trees and animals: Bristlecones, limber pines, and subalpine firs all live in this harsh environment and somehow cling to life in an area that is pounded by high winds and extreme weather. Last is the Arctic-Alpine Zone, which lies above timberline. This is an area where only the hardiest of plant and animal species can survive.

When I travel above timberline I am amazed to find that tundra grasses, small stunted wildflowers, pikas, summering elk, and bighorn sheep somehow seem to thrive in the summer months at this harsh altitude. It is a place where I respect all living things for their tenacious will to survive. Winter can start as early as September and last well into July.

Very few places in the United States can lay claim to such a diverse physical environment. This is indeed a special area, and I feel that all the hikes in this book are special. From the riparian ecosystem of Barr Lake State Park to the snow-capped summit of Grays Peak and everything in between, you can seek solitude in these lands. You can hike along wild mountain streams and hear the sound of mountain water, a sound that will calm your heart and lighten your spirit. You can sit on top of high mountain peaks and look in all directions, feeling that you can see to forever. You can wander through the aspens in fall, seeing and hearing their gold leaves quaking in a soft breeze. You can hike on a narrow mountain trail under a canopy of tall pine trees and see wild animals in their natural environment, or fish high alpine lakes under towering rocky peaks and hear the sound of solitude. Believe me, that is a beautiful sound. But most of all, with a little bit of effort and with strong legs and lungs, you can experience the natural world of Colorado's Front Range. Hopefully this book will help you get there.

Climate

Colorado's Front Range is blessed with brilliant weather and sees almost 300 days of sunshine. You can hike in Colorado's Front Range year-round. Summer can be hot, but all you have to do to escape the heat is travel to the high country. Winters are mild, and in high snow years you can strap on a pair of skis or snowshoes and experience the quiet that only winter brings. Spring and fall are times of stable weather and moderate temperatures. Summer in the high country is absolutely beautiful, and you should make it a point to travel and experience the beauty of the high mountain peaks.

Hiking with Children

One of the greatest joys my wife and I have had is the time we have spent with our three children in the woods. Hiking is a wonderful sport that can be enjoyed by the entire family. That said, things can go wrong with children when you are out in the woods, and they can go wrong very fast. Be prepared! Take extra clothing, food, diapers, water, and a healthy sense of humor.

Day hikes and shorter trails are the best for introducing your child to the outdoors. Your child's age and fitness level will dictate how many miles you travel in the woods. For toddlers, 1 to 4 miles will be just right. They are the hardest to travel with in the woods, and depending on how much or how long you want to carry them, your hike could be shorter. My son Jeremy had his own little backpack at the age of five and loved to carry his own food and water when we went into the woods. Older children travel at a faster rate and are strong enough to carry most of their gear. They require less attention and like to travel ahead of the adults, exploring on their own. Make sure the older children don't travel too far ahead and emphasize that they stay on the trail and wait for you at all trail junctions.

Younger children have a different agenda than most adults. They travel at a slower pace; they stop and check things out. Tree stumps, streams, butterflies, flowers, snow, and lakes are quite fascinating to their inquiring minds. They like to look at animals and bugs. Children will stop and sit down for no reason at all. They will ask a million questions. As a parent, enjoy your time with your children. Stop and answer all those questions. Sit with them on a log and treasure the time with your little ones in the woods; you won't regret it.

How to Use This Guide

This guide provides information on sixty hikes in the plains, foothills, and mountains of Colorado's Front Range. The hikes in this book range in length from 1 to 15 miles, with elevation gains ranging from as little as 100 feet to more than 3,000 feet. The trails vary from extremely rocky to flat and smooth. The hikes in this book start at an elevation of just over 5,000 feet, and go up to 14,000 feet above sea level. The hikes are presented from north to south, with Greyrock National Recreation Trail, just north of Fort Collins, being hike 1 and Waldo Canyon, just west of Colorado Springs being hike 60.

Each hike description begins with the highlights of the hike, outlining the physical, historical, and other special attractions that you may find along the way. Information is then given about the best season for the hike, how long the hike is, and the difficulty of the hike. Following that, you'll find a listing of the maps that you will need, the entity that manages the area, trail conditions, and directions to the trailhead. A detailed description of the hike is provided, followed by Miles and Directions, which details mileages between specific landmarks or trail junctions along the route.

A majority of the hikes in this book are day hikes and can easily be completed in a reasonable time frame. Almost all the hikes in this book could be turned into overnight excursions with the addition of a backpack, sleeping bag, tent, and other essentials. Make sure camping is allowed on the hike you are planning to do.

Read through the text and find the hike or hikes that best suit your needs. Distances are given for each hike and should be used as a reference point. Don't let the length of a hike stop you from doing that hike; go as far as you like on any given trail. If you are not up to completing a hike in this guide, turn around and return to the trailhead; come back another day. Just being outdoors and walking is enough for me.

Type of Trail

Suggested hikes have been categorized as follows:

Day hike: Best for a short excursion only, due to lack of either water or suitable camping sites.

Backpack: Best for backpacking with at least one or more nights in the backcountry. Many of the overnight hikes can be done as day hikes if you have the time and/or stamina.

Loop: Starts and finishes at the same trailhead with no (or very little) retracing of your steps. Sometimes the definition of a "loop" includes creative shapes (like a figure eight or lollipop) and a short walk on a dirt road to get you back to the trailhead.

Out-and-back: Traveling the same route coming and going.

Shuttle: A point-to-point trip that requires two vehicles (one left at each end of the trail) or a prearranged pickup at a designated time and place. One effective way to manage the logistical difficulties of shuttles is to arrange for a second party to start at the other end of the trail. The two parties then rendezvous at a predetermined time and place along the trail, trade keys, and drive to each other's home upon returning to the trailhead.

Difficulty Ratings

Difficulty ratings are inherently flawed: What's easy for you might be difficult for me. Still, such ratings serve as a general guide and give a useful approximation of a hike's challenge. Remember that ratings are not the final word, and that the most important factor is to be honest about your own fitness level when planning your trip. In this guidebook, difficulty ratings consider both how long and strenuous a hike is. Following are general guidelines for ratings:

Easy: Suitable for any hiker—young or old. Expect no serious elevation gain, hazards, or navigation problems.

Moderate: Suitable for hikers who have at least some experience and an average fitness level. Likely includes some elevation change and may have places where the trail is faint.

Strenuous: Suitable only for experienced hikers with above average fitness level. Possible hazardous trail sections, navigation difficulties, and serious elevation change.

Trail Mileage

Measuring trail distances is an inexact science at best. In this guidebook most distances have been taken from map measurements and from in-the-field estimates. Most trail signs on Colorado's Front Range do not include distances, and when they do you can bet they are just somebody else's best guess. Keep in mind that distance is often less important than difficulty. A steep 2-mile climb on rocky tread can take longer than a 4-mile stroll through a gentle river valley. It may be helpful to note that most hikers average about 2 miles per hour and take into consideration that what matters is not how far you go, it's how much you enjoy your time out on the trail.

Maps

The maps in this book serve as a general guide only. Don't hit the trail without buying a better, more detailed map. There are a few choices when it comes to maps, and they are listed with each hike.

Elevation Charts

All hike descriptions include elevation charts (except for five). Use these profiles to get a general picture of how much elevation gain and loss a hike entails. The charts are not meant to be a detailed, foot-by-foot account of the route, but serve as a quick glimpse of the overall elevation change.

Backcountry Regulations

- Get a wilderness permit for all overnight use (see Appendix A).
- Camp only in appropriate places (see Leave No Trace, below).
- Stay on trails (where possible) and don't create shortcuts.
- Dispose of human waste in a cat hole at least 200 feet from all water sources and campsites.
- Dispose of bathing and dishwater well away from water sources.
- Use camp stoves rather than cooking fires whenever possible.
- Carry out all trash. If you can pack it in, you can pack it out.
- Limit group size to ten or fewer.
- Suspend food out of reach of animals.
- Do not feed or in any way disturb the wildlife. Do not leave behind food scraps.
- Do not operate any mechanized vehicle in the wilderness.
- Do not destroy, deface, disturb, or remove from its natural setting any plant, rock, animal, or archaeological resource.

Please read about Leave No Trace for more details on minimizing impact on the wilderness.

Leave No Trace

Going into a wild area is like visiting a famous museum. You obviously do not want to leave your mark on an art treasure in the museum. If everybody going through the museum left one little mark, the piece of art would be quickly destroyed—and of what value is a big building full of trashed art? The same goes for pristine wild-lands. If we all left just one little mark on the landscape, the backcountry would soon be spoiled.

A wilderness can accommodate human use as long as everybody behaves. But a few thoughtless or uninformed visitors can ruin it for everybody who follows. All backcountry users have a responsibility to follow the rules of zero-impact camping.

Nowadays most wilderness users want to walk softly, but some aren't aware that they have poor manners. Often their actions are dictated by the outdated habits of a past generation of campers, who cut green boughs for evening shelters, built camp-fires with fire rings, and dug trenches around tents. In the 1950s, these practices may have been acceptable. But they leave long-lasting scars, and today such behavior is absolutely unacceptable.

Because wild places are becoming rare and the number of users is mushrooming, a code of ethics has grown out of the necessity of coping with the unending waves of people who want a perfect backcountry experience. Today, we all must leave no clues that we were there. Enjoy the wild, but don't leave any trace of your visit.

Leave No Trace

- Leave with everything you brought in.
- Leave no sign of your visit.
- Leave the landscape as you found it.

Most of us know better than to litter—in or out of the backcountry. Be sure you leave nothing, regardless of how small it is, along the trail or at your campsite. This means you should pack out everything, including orange peels, flip tops, cigarette butts, and gum wrappers. Also, pick up any trash that others leave behind.

Follow the main trail. Avoid cutting switchbacks and walking on vegetation beside the trail. Don't pick up "souvenirs," such as rocks, antlers, or wildflowers. The next person wants to see them, too, and collecting such souvenirs violates many regulations.

Avoid making loud noises on the trail (unless you are in bear country) or in camp. Be courteous—remember that sound travels easily in the backcountry, especially across water.

Carry a lightweight trowel to bury human waste 6 to 8 inches deep at least 200 feet from any water source. Pack out used toilet paper.

Go without a campfire. Carry a stove for cooking and a flashlight, candle lantern, or headlamp for light. For emergencies, learn how to build a no-trace fire.

Camp in obviously used sites when they are available. Otherwise, camp and cook on durable surfaces such as bedrock, sand, gravel bars, or bare ground.

Leave no trace—and put your ear to the ground and listen carefully. Thousands of people coming behind you are thanking you for your courtesy and good sense.

Backcountry Safety and Hazards

The Boy Scouts of America have been guided for decades by what is perhaps the single best piece of safety advice—Be prepared! For starters, this means carrying survival and first-aid materials, proper clothing, a compass, and a topographic map—and knowing how to use them.

Perhaps the second-best piece of safety advice is to tell somebody where you're going and when you plan to return. Pilots must file flight plans before every trip, and anybody venturing into a blank spot on the map should do the same. File your "flight plan" with a friend or relative before taking off.

Close behind your flight plan and being prepared with proper equipment is physical conditioning. Being fit not only makes wilderness travel more fun, it makes it safer. Here are a few more tips:

- Check the weather forecast. Be careful not to get caught at high altitude by a bad storm or along a stream in a flash flood. Watch cloud formations closely so you don't get stranded on a ridgeline during a lightning storm. Avoid traveling during prolonged periods of cold weather.
- Avoid traveling alone in the wilderness and keep your party together.
- Don't exhaust yourself or other members of your party by traveling too far or too fast. Let the slowest person set the pace.
- Study basic survival and first aid before leaving home.
- Before you leave for the trailhead, find out as much as you can about the route, especially the potential hazards.
- Don't wait until you're confused to look at your maps. Follow them as you go along, so you have a continual fix on your location.
- If you get lost, don't panic. Sit down and relax for a few minutes while you carefully check your topo map and take a compass reading. Confidently plan your next move. It's often smart to retrace your steps until you find familiar ground, even if you think it might lengthen your trip. Lots of people get temporarily lost in the wilderness and survive—usually by calmly and rationally dealing with the situation.
- Stay clear of all wild animals.
- Take a first-aid kit that includes, at a minimum, a sewing needle, snake-bite kit, aspirin, antibacterial ointment, antiseptic swabs, butterfly bandages, adhesive tape, adhesive strips, gauze pads, two triangular bandages, codeine tablets, two inflatable splints, moleskin for blisters, 3-inch gauze, CPR shield, rubber gloves, and lightweight first-aid instructions.
- Take a survival kit that includes, at a minimum, a compass, whistle, matches in a waterproof container, cigarette lighter, candle, signal mirror, flashlight, fire starter, aluminum foil, water purification tablets, space blanket, and flare.

Finally, don't forget that knowledge is the best defense against unexpected hazards.

Lightning: You Might Never Know What Hit You

Mountains are prone to sudden thunderstorms. If you get caught in a lightning storm, take special precautions.

- Lightning can travel ahead of a storm, so take cover before the storm hits.
- Don't try to make it back to your vehicle. It isn't worth the risk. Instead, seek shelter even if it's only a short way back to the trailhead. Lightning storms usually don't last long, and from a safe vantage point, you might enjoy the sights and sounds.
- Be especially careful not to get caught on a mountaintop or an exposed ridge; under large, solitary trees; in the open; or near standing water.
- Seek shelter in a low-lying area, ideally in a stand of small, uniformly sized trees.
- Avoid anything that attracts lightning, like metal tent poles, graphite fishing rods, or pack frames.
- Crouch with both feet firmly on the ground.
- If you have a pack (without a metal frame) or a sleeping pad with you, put your feet on it for extra insulation against shock.
- Don't walk or huddle together. Instead, stay 50 feet apart, so if somebody gets hit by lightning, others in your party can give first aid.
- If you're in a tent, stay in your sleeping bag with your feet on your sleeping pad.

Hypothermia: The Silent Killer

Be aware of hypothermia—a condition in which the body's internal temperature drops below normal. It can lead to mental and physical collapse and death.

Hypothermia is caused by exposure to cold and is aggravated by wetness, wind, and exhaustion. The moment you begin to lose heat faster than your body produces it, you're suffering from exposure. Your body starts involuntary exercise, such as shivering, to stay warm and makes involuntary adjustments to preserve normal temperature in vital organs, restricting blood flow in the extremities. Both responses drain your energy reserves. The only way to stop the drain is to reduce the degree of exposure.

With full-blown hypothermia, as energy reserves are exhausted, cold blood reaches the brain, depriving you of good judgment and reasoning power. You won't be aware that this is happening. You will lose control of your hands. Your internal temperature will slide downward. Without treatment, this slide leads to stupor, collapse, and death.

To defend against hypothermia, stay dry. When clothes get wet, they lose about 90 percent of their insulating value. Wool loses relatively less heat; cotton, down, and some synthetics lose more. Choose rain clothes that cover the head, neck, body, and legs and provide good protection against wind-driven rain. Most hypothermia cases develop in air temperatures between 30 and 50 degrees Fahrenheit, but hypothermia can develop in warmer temperatures.

If your party is exposed to wind, cold, and wet, watch yourself and others for uncontrollable fits of shivering; vague, slow, slurred speech; memory lapses; incoherence; immobile, fumbling hands; frequent stumbling or a lurching gait; drowsiness; apparent exhaustion; and inability to get up after a rest. When a member of your party has hypothermia, he or she may deny any problem. Believe the symptoms, not the victim. Even mild symptoms demand the following treatment:

- Get the victim out of the wind and rain.
- Strip off all wet clothes.
- If the victim is only mildly impaired, give him or her warm drinks. Then get the victim in warm clothes and a warm sleeping bag. Place well-wrapped water bottles filled with heated water close to the victim.
- If the victim is badly impaired, attempt to keep him or her awake. Put the victim in a sleeping bag with another person—both naked. If you have a double bag, put two warm people in with the victim.

Fording Rivers

Early summer hiking in the mountains of Colorado's Front Range may involve crossing streams swollen with runoff. When done correctly and carefully, crossing a big river can be safe, but you must know your limits.

Know those cases where you simply should turn back. Even if only one member of your party (such as a child) might not be able to follow larger, stronger members, you might not want to try a risky ford. Never be embarrassed by being too cautious.

One key to safely fording rivers is confidence. If you aren't a strong swimmer, you should be. This not only allows you to safely get across a river that is a little deeper and stronger than you thought, but it gives you the confidence to avoid panic. Just like getting lost, panic can easily make the situation worse.

Practice builds confidence. Find a warm-water river near your home and carefully practice crossing it both with a pack and without. You can also start with a smaller stream and work up to a major river. After you've become a strong swimmer, get used to swimming in the current.

When you get to the ford, carefully assess the situation. Don't automatically cross at the point where the trail comes to the stream and head on a straight line for the marker on the other side. A mountain river can change every spring during high runoff, so a ford that was safe last year might be too deep this year. Study upstream and downstream and look for a place where the stream widens and the water is not over waist deep on the shortest member of your party. The tail end of an island is usually a good place, as is a long riffle. The inside of a meander sometimes makes a safe ford, but in other cases a long, shallow section can be followed by a short, deep section next to the outside of the bend where the current picks up speed and carves out a deep channel.

Before starting any serious ford, make sure your matches, camera, billfold, clothes, sleeping bag, and other items you must keep dry are in watertight bags.

On Colorado's Front Range, most streams are cold, so have dry clothes ready when you get to the other side to minimize the risk of hypothermia, especially on a cold, rainy day.

Minimize the amount of time you spend in the water, but don't rush across. Instead, go slowly and deliberately, taking one step at a time, being careful to get each foot securely planted before lifting the other foot. Take a 45-degree angle instead of going straight across, following a riffle line if possible.

Don't ford with bare feet. Wear hiking boots without the socks, sneakers, or tightly strapped sandals. In an emergency, wool socks pulled over rubber soles provide a good grip on the slippery rock.

Keep sideways to the current. Turning upstream or downstream increases the current's force.

In some cases, two or three people can cross together, locking forearms, with the strongest person on the upstream side.

When in mountainous terrain, and if you have a choice, ford in the early morning when the stream isn't as deep. The cool nighttime temperatures slow snow melt and reduce the water flow into the rivers.

On small streams, a sturdy walking stick used on the upstream side for balance helps prevent a fall, but in a major river with a fast current, a walking stick offers little help.

Loosen the belt and straps on your pack. If you fall or get washed downstream, a waterlogged pack can anchor you to the bottom, so you must be able to easily release your pack.

If you're 6' 4" and a strong swimmer, you might feel secure crossing a big river, but you might have children or smaller hikers in your party. In this case, the strongest person can cross first and string a line across the river to aid those who follow. This line (with the help of a carabiner) can also be used to float packs across instead of taking the chance of a waterlogged pack dragging you under. (If you knew about the ford in advance, you could pack a lightweight rubber raft or inner tube for this purpose.) Depending on your size and strength, you might also want to carry children.

Be prepared for the worst. Sometimes circumstances arise where you simply must cross instead of going back, even though the ford looks dangerous. Also, you can underestimate the depth of the channel or strength of the current, especially after a thunderstorm when a muddy river hides its true depth. In these cases, whether you like it or not, you might be swimming. If this happens, don't panic, and do not try to swim directly across. Instead, pick a long angle and gradually cross to the other side, taking as much as 100 yards or more to finally get across. If your pack starts to drag you down, release it immediately, even if you have to abandon it. If you lose control and get washed downstream, go feet first, so you don't hit your head on rocks or logs.

Be sure to report any dangerous ford to a ranger as soon as you finish your trip.

Be Mountain Lion Alert

You're sure to see plenty of deer along Colorado's Front Range, which means mountain lions probably aren't far away. Cougars feed on deer and elk, and the rugged, rocky areas along Colorado's Front Range constitute some of the best cougar habitat in the West. Although many people consider themselves lucky indeed to see a mountain lion in the wild, the big cats—nature's perfect predator—are potentially dangerous. Attacks on humans are extremely rare, but it's wise to educate yourself before heading into mountain lion habitat.

To stay as safe as possible when hiking in mountain lion country, follow this advice:

- Travel with a friend or group, and stay together.
- Don't let small children wander away by themselves.
- Don't let pets run unleashed.
- Avoid hiking at dawn and dusk, when mountain lions are most active.
- Know how to behave if you encounter a mountain lion.

In the vast majority of mountain lion encounters, the animals exhibit avoidance, indifference, or curiosity that never results in human injury. But it is natural to be alarmed if you have an encounter of any kind. Try to keep your cool and consider the following:

Recognize threatening mountain lion behavior. A few cues may help you gauge the risk of attack. If a mountain lion is more than 50 yards away, and it directs its attention to you, it may be only curious. This situation represents only a slight risk for adults but a more serious risk to unaccompanied children. At this point, you should move away, while keeping the animal in your peripheral vision. Also, look for rocks, sticks, or something to use as a weapon, just in case.

If a mountain lion is crouched and staring at you less than 50 yards away, it may be assessing the chances of a successful attack. If this behavior continues, the risk of attack may be high.

Do not approach a mountain lion. Give the animal the opportunity to move on. Slowly back away, but maintain eye contact if close. Mountain lions are not known to attack humans to defend young or a kill, but they have been reported to "charge" in rare instances and may want to stay in the area. It's best to choose another route or time to hike through the area.

Do not run from a mountain lion. Running may stimulate a predatory response.

Make noise. If you encounter a mountain lion, be vocal and talk or yell loudly and regularly. Try not to panic. Shout to make others in the area aware of the situation.

Maintain eye contact. Eye contact presents a challenge to the mountain lion, showing you are aware of its presence. Eye contact also helps you know where it is. However, if the behavior of the mountain lion is not threatening (if it is, for example, grooming or periodically looking away), maintain visual contact through your peripheral vision and move away.

Appear larger than you are. Raise your arms above your head and make steady waving motions. Raise your jacket or another object above your head. Do not bend over, as this will make you appear smaller and more "preylike."

If you are with small children, pick them up. Bring children close to you, maintain eye contact with the mountain lion, and pull the children up without bending over. If you are with other children or adults, band together.

Defend yourself and others. If attacked, fight back. Try to remain standing. Do not feign death. Pick up a branch or rock; pull out a knife, pepper spray, or other deterrent device. Individuals have fended off mountain lions with rocks, tree limbs, and even cameras. Keep in mind this is a last effort and defending pets is not recommended.

Respect any warning signs posted by agencies.

Teach others in your group how to behave in case of a mountain lion encounter.

Report encounters. Record your location and the details of any encounter and notify the nearest landowner or land management agency. The land management agency (federal, state, or county) may want to visit the site and, if appropriate, post education/warning signs. Fish and wildlife agencies should also be notified because they record and track such encounters. If physical injury occurs, it is important to leave the area and not disturb the site of attack. Mountain lions that have attacked people must be killed, and an undisturbed site is critical for effectively locating the dangerous mountain lion.

Be Bear Aware

The first step of any hike in bear country is an attitude adjustment. Being prepared for bears doesn't only mean having the right equipment. It also means having the right information. Black bears along Colorado's Front Range do not, as a rule, attack humans, but they may pose a danger if you handle your food improperly. At the very least, letting a bear get human food is like contributing—directly—to the eventual destruction of that bear. Think of proper bear etiquette as protecting the bears as much as you.

Camping in Bear Country

Staying overnight in bear country is not dangerous, but the presence of food, cooking, and garbage adds an additional risk to your trip. Bears are usually most active at night, as well. Following a few basic practices greatly minimizes the chance of encounter.

To be as safe as possible, store everything that has any food smell. Ziplock bags are perfect for reducing food smell and help keep food from spilling on your pack, clothing, or other gear. If a food item spills on your clothes, change into other clothes for sleeping and hang clothes with food smells out of reach, with the food and garbage. If you take them into the tent, you aren't separating your sleeping area from food smells. Try to keep food odors off your pack, but if you fail, put the food bag inside and hang the pack.

Be sure to finalize your food storage plans before it gets dark. It's not only difficult to store food after darkness falls, it's easier to forget some juicy morsel on the ground.

Bear cub

Store food in airtight, sturdy, waterproof bags to prevent food odors from circulating throughout the forest. You can purchase dry bags at most outdoor specialty stores, but you can get by with a trash compactor bag. Don't use regular garbage bags because they can break easily.

See the diagrams that follow for different ways to hang a bear bag. If you have two bags to hang, divide your food into two equal sacks. Use a stone to toss the end of a piece of nylon cord (parachute cord is fine; under most circumstances there is no need for the heavier stuff) over the limb well out from the trunk, then tie half your food to the end. Pull the food up to the limb, then tie your remaining food sack onto the cord as high as you can reach. Stuff the excess cord into the food sack, then use a stick to push the second sack several feet higher than your head. The first sack will act as a counterweight and descend a few feet, but it should remain at least as high as the second sack. In the morning, use a stick to pull down one of the sacks.

Don't get paranoid about the types of food you bring—all food has some smell. By consciously reducing the number of dishes (pack out all food scraps), as well as the amount of packaging, and by consuming everything on your plate, as well as paying careful attention to storage, you will make your backpacking culinary experience not only more enjoyable and hassle-free for yourself, but also more bear-proof.

Remember Rattlesnakes

Rattlesnakes strike humans only out of self-defense, when they're startled or otherwise afraid. The solution, of course, is to avoid scaring them. Look where you place your feet and hands when hiking in rattlesnake country (which includes most of the trails in *Hiking Colorado's Front Range,* but especially those at lower, warmer elevations).

If you do encounter a rattlesnake, slowly back away and give it a chance to go away. Almost invariably it will seize the opportunity and slither away. If it doesn't, simply give the snake a wide berth and leave well enough alone. Do not throw rocks or sticks at it.

If bitten by a rattlesnake, don't panic. Rattlesnake bites are rarely fatal to healthy adults. Use a snakebite kit immediately to extract as much of the venom as possible. (It may actually be a "dry bite," in which no venom is delivered—intended only to frighten you.) Do not run or otherwise speed up your circulation, as that increases the spread of the venom in your bloodstream. Keep the bite site lower than your heart to slow the spread of venom. Seek medical attention as soon as possible.

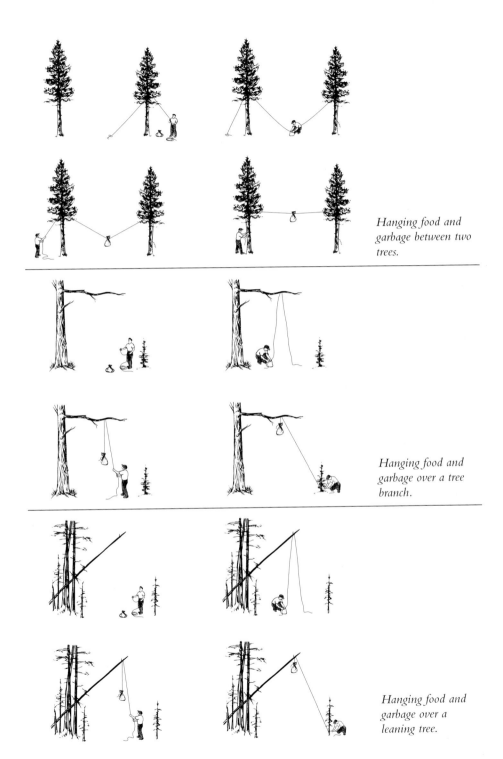

Hanging food and garbage between two trees.

Hanging food and garbage over a tree branch.

Hanging food and garbage over a leaning tree.

Map Legend

Transportation

≡(25)≡ Interstate Highway

≡(40)≡ US Highway

≡(119)≡ State Highway

≡[94]≡ Local/ County/Forest Road

= = = = Unimproved Road

- - - - - - Featured Trail

- - - - - - Trail

+—+—+ Railroad

Water Features

Body of Water

River/Creek

Intermittent Creek

Waterfall

Land Management

National Park/
Forest Boundary

State/Local/
Open Space Park

— · — · Continental Divide

Symbols

|||||||| Boardwalk

▲ Campground

▲ Campsite

→ Direction Arrow

⊕ Hospital

🅿 Parking

▲ Peak/Summit

⊞ Picnic Area

■ Point of Interest/Structure

🏠 Ranger Station

🚻 Restroom

🎿 Ski Area

🐎 Stable

🗼 Tower

○ Town

① Trailhead

🔭 Viewpoint/Overlook

❓ Visitor Center/Information Center

Fort Collins Area

1 Greyrock National Recreation Trail

This is a beautiful hike up into some very wild country high above the Cache la Poudre River. Wildlife, views, and a steep grunt up a narrow gulch to a beautiful open meadow are the highlights on this hike. Wildflowers abound in Greyrock Meadow during the early summer months.

Start: From the parking area, cross CO 14 and then cross a bridge to the start of the well marked Greyrock National Recreation Trail.
Distance: 5.9-mile loop
Hiking time: About 2.5 to 4 hours
Difficulty: Moderate to strenuous
Trail surface: Rocky

Seasons: Year-round, depending on snowfall
Other trail users: Equestrians
Canine compatibility: Dogs permitted
Maps: Trails Illustrated/Cache la Poudre/ Big Thompson #101
Trail contact: Roosevelt National Forest; (970) 295-6600

Finding the trailhead: From Fort Collins, travel north on US 287 to CO 14. Travel west on CO 14 up Poudre Canyon for 8.2 miles to the Greyrock National Recreation Trail trailhead and parking area on the left. GPS: N40 69.5278' / W105 28.5278'

The Hike

From the parking area, drop down the steps and cross CO 14. Use caution. Follow the trail across the bridge and arrive at the start of the Greyrock National Recreation Trail.

Go left, up along the Cache la Poudre River through thickets, willows, tall grasses, yuccas, and ponderosa pines. The trail climbs at a nice grade and goes to the right, up a narrow gulch away from the river. Continue climbing through the trees up to a trail junction at around the 0.6-mile mark.

The Greyrock Trail goes to the right and the Greyrock Meadow Trail goes to the left. This hike takes the Greyrock Trail and heads up into a very narrow gulch. Follow the tight trail through a rocky section, climbing a steep grade. Large rocks cover the steep hillsides of the trail, as do beautiful ponderosa pines and various wildflowers.

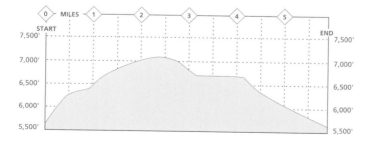

Greyrock National Recreation Trail

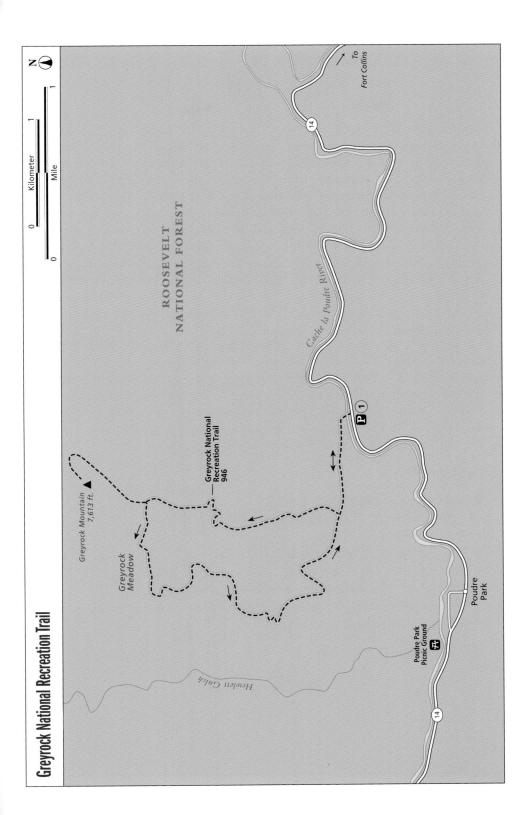

N

Kilometer
0   1
Mile
0   1

ROOSEVELT
NATIONAL FOREST

Greyrock Mountain
7,613 ft. ▲

Greyrock
Meadow

Greyrock National
Recreation Trail
946

Hewlett Gulch

Cache la Poudre River

Poudre Park
Picnic Ground

Poudre
Park

14

14

P 1

To
Fort Collins

The trail climbs a short distance to the left. then climbs back right, up to a small seasonal creek. Cross the creek and climb several short switchbacks; the trail is now on the right of the drainage. Aspen trees appear and blend in nicely with the tall pine trees.

The trail becomes level and travels up past several large ponderosa trees. At around the 1.7-mile mark the trail switches back and forth over the gulch and then makes a left away from the gulch across a steep hillside. Several burned trees line the trail, probably the victims of a lightning strike. There are excellent views to the south, and you can look down the gulch and see the substantial elevation gain you have made.

Reach a cluster of rocks, enjoy the views, and take a break. Continue by following the trail up through several rocks near the path. Catch a glimpse of Greyrock Mountain's granite walls, and arrive at a trail junction in an open meadow. Go left on the Greyrock Meadow Trail, through a beautiful meadow and then back into the trees.

The trail drops down on rocky tread into the wide, beautiful Greyrock Meadow. It then slices across the meadow, with large, granite rocks clinging to the steep hillsides. There is a great view back to Greyrock Mountain, and the meadow is filled with wildflowers during the summer months.

The trail goes left into the trees and climbs through several rocky sections to a ridge. It pops out of the trees and begins a steep descent down an open hillside. The trail takes several long switchbacks and then plunges into a narrow gulch. Follow the trail into the gulch and drainage. Willows, aspens, and wildflowers grow close to the drainage, and are quite a contrast to the steep hill you just descended.

Arrive back at the first trail junction and continue straight to the footbridge. Cross the bridge and highway and climb the steps back to the parking area.

Miles and Directions

0.0 Start by descending the steps.

0.6 The trail forks. Go right on the Greyrock National Recreation Trail 946.

1.3 Cross a small stream.

2.2 Arrive at a trail junction and views of Greyrock Mountain.

2.9 Arrive at Greyrock Meadow.

3.5 Reach an overlook with great views to the north and to Greyrock.

5.2 Return to the first trail junction. Retrace your route back to the trailhead and parking lot.

5.9 Arrive back at the trailhead and parking area.

2 Arthur's Rock

Wonderful hiking in a beautiful state park just west of Fort Collins. This loop takes you up to Arthur's Rock, traveling over beautiful flower-filled hills, with views to the east of Horsetooth Reservoir, south to Horsetooth Mountain Park, and east to the plains. A great wildlife hike and a good place to bring the family and enjoy all the activities this park has to offer.

Start: From the parking area, pass the kiosk heading west to reach the signed Arthur's Rock Trail.
Distance: 3.6 miles out and back
Hiking time: About 2 to 3 hours
Difficulty: Moderate
Trail surface: Rocky
Seasons: Year-round

Other trail users: Equestrians
Canine compatibility: None
Maps: USGS Horsetooth Reservoir CO; Lory State Park map
Trail contact: Colorado State Parks; (970) 493-4104; http://www.parks.state.co.us/parks/lory/Pages/LoryStatePark.aspx

Finding the trailhead: Head north on US 287 from Fort Collins, following the signs for Lory State Park. About 5 miles north of Fort Collins, just past the town of Laporte, turn left on CR 54E. Getting to the park is half the fun. Look for CR 25E. Go left on CR 25E, cutting to the left. Follow CR 25E to CR 23. Go right on CR 23 to CR 25G, which leads into Lory State Park. Pay the entrance fee and travel 2 miles to the Arthur's Rock trailhead and parking area. GPS: N40 56.6602' / W105 18.3324'

The Hike

From the trailhead, go west past the restrooms and (very informative) kiosk on the Arthur's Rock Trail. Cross a wood footbridge and head left across another footbridge and into a narrow gulch. Follow the narrow, rocky trail up through the mouth of the gulch. The trail climbs several switchbacks, gaining altitude, and comes to a junction with the Overlook Trail in an open meadow. Wildflowers, tall grass, ponderosas, a great view of Arthur's Rock, and a cluster of cottonwoods on the right all add to the natural beauty of this wonderful spot.

Continue straight on the Arthur's Rock Trail through the meadow to a trail junction at the 0.6-mile mark. Continue straight into the ponderosas and enjoy beautiful hiking under a canopy of these stately trees.

The trail comes out of the trees, crosses a seasonal drainage, and then climbs steeply up the side of an open hill to an overlook at the 1.3-mile mark. Go right for great views of Horsetooth Reservoir and the plains. Follow the trail along the base of Arthur's Rock on narrow tread; yuccas and cacti grow on the steep, sunny slope on the left.

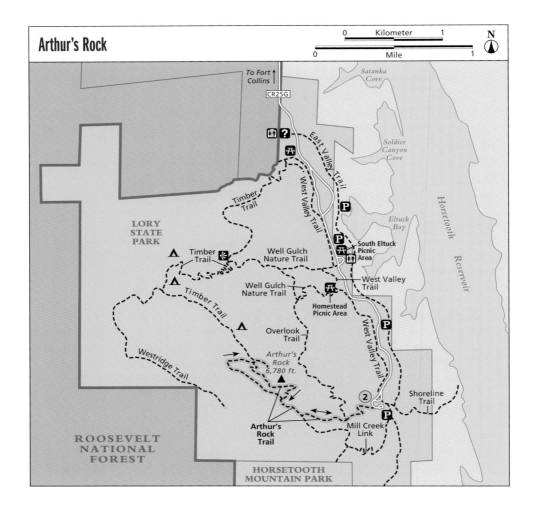

Arthur's Rock

0   Kilometer   1

0   Mile   1

N

Satanka Cove

To Fort Collins ↑

CR25G

East Valley Trail

West Valley Trail

Soldier Canyon Cove

Timber Trail

LORY STATE PARK

Timber Trail

Well Gulch Nature Trail

Eltuck Bay

South Eltuck Picnic Area

West Valley Trail

Well Gulch Nature Trail

Homestead Picnic Area

Horsetooth

Reservoir

Timber Trail

Overlook Trail

West Valley Trail

Westridge Trail

Arthur's Rock 6,780 ft.

2

Shoreline Trail

Arthur's Rock Trail

Mill Creek Link

ROOSEVELT NATIONAL FOREST

HORSETOOTH MOUNTAIN PARK

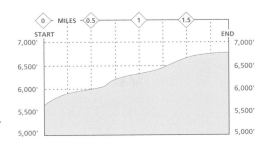

The trail climbs rapidly and cuts past a tall, pointed boulder and through a narrow passage up to a junction with the Timber Trail at the 1.7-mile mark. Take a short break to soak in the views. To the east and running in a north-south direction, sandstone hogbacks are visible and reveal movements of the earth millions of years ago. Two of the earth's plates moved in an east-west direction. Where they hit each other, the edges of the plates were pushed upward from deep in the earth's core. Millions of years later, and with the help of wind, sun, snow, and rain, what was once deep underground now lies exposed.

Go right and follow the trail down to the east. Then go left, up a steep, rock-filled gully, and gain a flat area and the top of Arthur's Rock. Enjoy the spectacular views to the north, east, and south. Use caution on the top of the rocks and limit the amount of scrambling you do on these steep rocks with big drop-offs.

Retrace your route back to the overlook at the 1.3-mile mark. For a different return go left past the sign and drop down the Overlook Trail. The trail drops at a rapid rate and soon comes to a junction with the Homestead Trail. Continue down on the Overlook Trail, cross a small drainage, and meet the Arthur's Rock Trail. Go left on the Arthur's Rock Trail for 0.3 mile and arrive back at the trailhead.

Miles and Directions

0.0   Start by passing the restrooms and information kiosk.

0.3   Overlook Trail junction.

1.3   Overlook on the right.

1.7   Junction with Timber Trail.

1.8   Arrive at the summit of Arthur's Rock; enjoy the views.

3.6   Arrive back at the trailhead.

3 Horsetooth Falls Loop

A beautiful hike leads up to a cascading waterfall on a trail through open hills, narrow gulches, open meadows, and rock-lined ridges. The best time of the year to do the hike is late spring, when the wildflowers are blooming and the falls are quite impressive with water from the spring runoff.

Start: From the kiosk, walk north to reach the signed Soderberg Trail.
Distance: 3.4-mile loop
Hiking time: About 1.5 to 2.5 hours
Difficulty: Moderate
Trail surface: Rocky
Seasons: Year-round (best in late spring)

Other trail users: Mountain bikers and equestrians
Canine compatibility: Dogs must be on leash
Maps: USGS Horsetooth Reservoir; Horsetooth Mountain Park
Trail contact: Larimer County Parks and Open Space; (970) 498-7000; www.larimer .org/naturalresources/

Finding the trailhead: From US 287 and Harmony Avenue in Fort Collins, go west on Harmony Avenue (CR 38E) for 8.7 miles to the entrance of Horsetooth Mountain Park, the trailhead, and parking. GPS: N40 32.3384' / W105 10.4299'

The Hike

Grab a Horsetooth Falls Discovery Trail map from the kiosk. This is a great map to have; it explains the geology, wildlife, and history of the area.

Head to the north and past the last picnic area to reach the start of the Soderberg Trail. Go through the gate and angle to the right on a narrow trail. Climb up past the first interpretive post and reach an open hillside. Head north to a lone ponderosa tree on the right and a junction with the Horsetooth Falls Trail.

Go right on the Horsetooth Falls Trail and drop down past thickets, yuccas, and scrub oak to a narrow gulch. Look north on the steep hillside for mule deer, which like the grass-covered hillside. Head west, up the gulch, to a wood footbridge across Spring Creek. Climb steeply up wood and rock steps to a junction with the Spring Creek Trail at the 1.2-mile mark. Go left on Horsetooth Falls Trail and down to the falls.

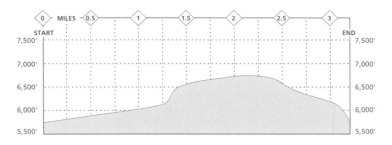

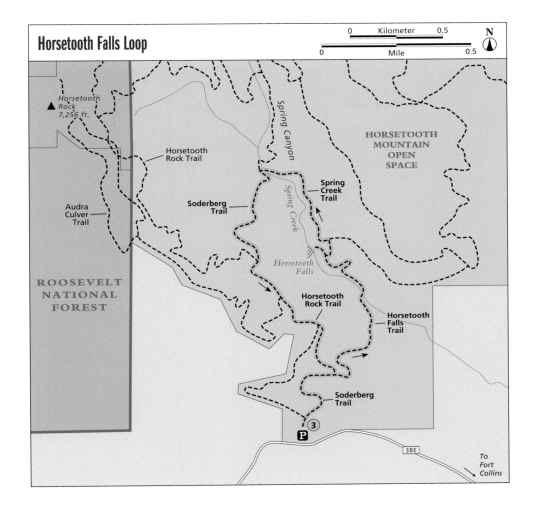

0 Kilometer 0.5

N

0 Mile 0.5

Horsetooth Rock
7,256 ft.

Horsetooth
Rock Trail

Spring Canyon

Spring Creek
Trail

HORSETOOTH
MOUNTAIN
OPEN
SPACE

Soderberg
Trail

Audra
Culver
Trail

Spring Creek

Horsetooth
Falls

ROOSEVELT
NATIONAL
FOREST

Horsetooth
Rock Trail

Horsetooth
Falls
Trail

Soderberg
Trail

3

P

38E

To
Fort
Collins

Relax and enjoy the sounds of the tumbling waters. A bench is located off the trail and makes a great place to hang out and enjoy the scenery. When you are rested, turn around and go back to the Spring Creek Trail.

Go left up the Spring Creek Trail and climb steeply above the falls. Respect all of the trail closures and stay on the main trail. Reach a level area and traverse across the side of a steep hill covered with tall ponderosas, yuccas, cacti, and wildflowers. Reach the seventh interpretive sign. Continue straight toward a junction with the Soderberg Trail.

At around the 1.8-mile mark reach the Soderberg Trail. Relax at this beautiful spot. The cool waters of Spring Creek flow by, wildflowers grow along the creekside, and tall rocks surround you on the steep hillsides. Go left on the Soderberg Trail, and climb up through a beautiful stand of ponderosas. Reach an open meadow on the left. The trail becomes wider, and stands of young ponderosas line the trail.

Climb to a hill point, passing the Horsetooth Rock and Audra Culver Trails. There are great views to the east and north. Take the hiker's trail that drops steeply to the Horsetooth Falls Trail. Go right, and retrace your route back to the trailhead to finish the loop.

Miles and Directions

0.0 Start by picking up the Soderberg Trail past the last picnic area.

0.4 Go right on Horsetooth Falls Trail.

1.3 Arrive at Horsetooth Falls.

1.8 Arrive at a junction with the Soderberg Trail; go left.

2.6 Continue straight on the Soderberg Trail.

2.7 Continue straight on the Soderberg Trail.

2.9 Arrive at a trail junction, continue straight on the Soderberg Trail.

3.0 Continue straight on the Soderberg Trail.

3.4 Arrive back at the trailhead.

4 Dome Mountain Trail

A strenuous hike that climbs up to the summit of Sheep Mountain (8,450 feet), high above the Big Thompson River and Canyon. The trail is well marked with mileage markers and informative signs pointing out information on plant life, erosions, and geology.

Start: From the parking area, access the Dome Mountain Trail near the kiosk.
Distance: 9.0 miles out and back
Hiking time: About 4 to 5 hours
Difficulty: Moderate to strenuous
Trail surface: Varies between very smooth in some sections to extremely rocky in others
Seasons: Apr to Nov
Other trail users: None

Canine compatibility: Dogs must be under control
Maps: Trails Illustrated Cache la Poudre-Big Thompson #101
Trail contact: Roosevelt National Forest and the city of Loveland; (970) 295-6600; www .fs.usda.gov/contactus/arp/about-forest/ contactus

Finding the trailhead: From the junction of US 287 and US 34 in Loveland, travel west on US 34 for 14 miles into Big Thompson Canyon, to the Dome Mountain Trailhead on the left. The hike starts at a gate near the restrooms. GPS: N40 25.2787' / W105 17.2069'

The Hike

From the parking area, follow the road up past a gate to a sign pointing to the summit trail. Make a quick left and go up to a second sign near a large pipe on the left. Go left again here; the trail becomes narrow as it clings to the side of a steep hill.

Begin a steep climb to where the trail cuts across a talus slope. Read the first of many informative signs that are located along the trail. This section of the trail travels through a forest of beautiful ponderosa pines and the occasional Douglas fir. Along the trail pointed yuccas and pricklypear cacti grow alongside delicate blooming wildflowers.

The trail switches back steeply in a west-to-east direction, with nice views in both directions. Soon you arrive at the 1-mile marker, with open views to the east. The trail becomes quite steep as you continue to climb high above a narrow gulch that is to the left.

The terrain stays rocky and continues to switchback up and up. Arrive at the 2-mile marker and begin the steepest section of the hike. The trail becomes quite narrow and very rocky as it travels through a beautiful forest of mature ponderosa pines and weird rock formations. Slide through a natural rock corridor and begin a slight descent to a spring, on the right just before the 3-mile marker. This is a good spot for a rest.

Dome Mountain Trail

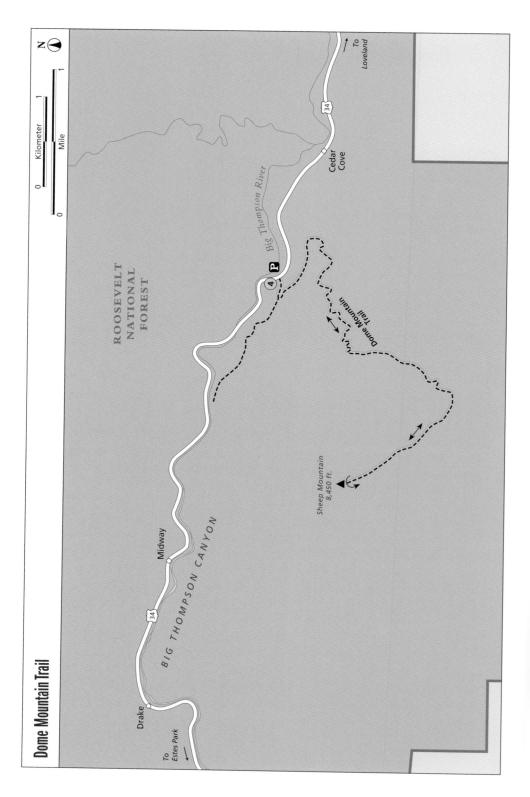

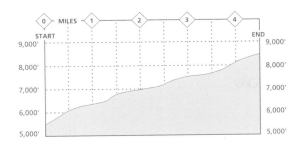

At the 3-mile marker the trail stays fairly level and actually drops a bit into a beautiful aspen forest with a small drainage. What a relief from all that climbing! Enjoy nice hiking through the aspen, with views to the north and west of Sheep Mountain.

Arrive at the 4-mile marker and cruise up through the rocks to the summit of Sheep Mountain. Enjoy views to the north, and of Loveland and the plains to the east.

After a well-deserved rest, retrace your route back to the trailhead.

Miles and Directions

0.0 Start by passing the gate.

0.2 Go left up a narrow trail.

0.4 Go left, climbing up a steep hill.

0.6 Cross a talus slope.

1.0 Pass a mile marker.

2.0 Pass a mile marker.

2.5 Pass through a natural rock corridor.

2.9 Reach the spring.

3.0 Pass a mile marker.

3.5 Reach the aspen forest.

4.0 Pass a mile marker.

4.5 Arrive at the summit of Sheep Mountain. Retrace your steps.

9.0 Arrive back at the trailhead.

5 Devil's Backbone Nature Trail

A nice family hike follows along the base of the Devil's Backbone just west of Loveland.

Start: From the parking lot, walk north on a road to reach the signed Devil's Backbone Nature Trail.
Distance: 2.7-mile loop
Hiking time: About 1.5 to 2.5 hours
Difficulty: Easy
Trail surface: Smooth
Seasons: Year-round

Other trail users: Mountain bikers and equestrians
Canine compatibility: Dogs must be on leash
Maps: USGS Larimer County CO;Larimer County Open Space/Devil's Backbone map
Trail contact: Larimer County Parks and Open Lands; (970) 498-7000; www.larimer .org/naturalresources/

Finding the trailhead: From the intersection of US 287 and US 34 in Loveland, go west on US 34 for 4.8 miles to Glade Road. Turn right on Glade Road and make an immediate right turn on Wild Lane. Travel 0.3 mile on Wild Lane to the Devil's Backbone Trailhead and parking area. GPS: N40 24.4237' / W105 09.0802'

The Hike

From the parking area, travel north up to the kiosk. Grab a Devil's Backbone Nature Trail map. The map explains local history, geology, flora, and wildlife surrounding the Devil's Backbone area.

Past the kiosk, the trail follows a road leading to the Wild Lane Bed and Breakfast. Go right just before the bed-and-breakfast, following the sign for the Devil's Backbone Trail, up to a gate. Stay right of the gate and curve around the side of a small hill, with an irrigation ditch on your left and a house down to the right.

Cross two wood footbridges at the 0.3-mile point and climb a small hill toward a trail junction. There are good views to the north, and in the early summer months yuccas, lupines, and other wildflowers bloom on the east-facing hill. Continue north.

Arrive at a trail junction; for this hike go right. The Devil's Backbone Nature Trail travels through a nice area of mahogany oak, cacti, and hills filled with yuccas. At around the 1-mile mark a good view of Devil's Backbone can be seen to the west.

Continue north up to a trail junction at the 1.3-mile mark, where a new trail and loop continue to the north and east. For this hike, go left on the Devil's Backbone Nature Trail and angle back to the south and up toward the Keyhole (a keyhole-shaped rock formation caused by erosion). Arrive at the Keyhole and a metal post marked 6. Time to bring out the map and read about how the Keyhole was formed.

Follow the trail along Devil's Backbone, keeping your map handy for quick reference. Reach a metal post marked 5 at the 1.7-mile mark. Learn who used to roam these lands millions of years ago. The trail crests a small hill at the 1.8-mile mark and

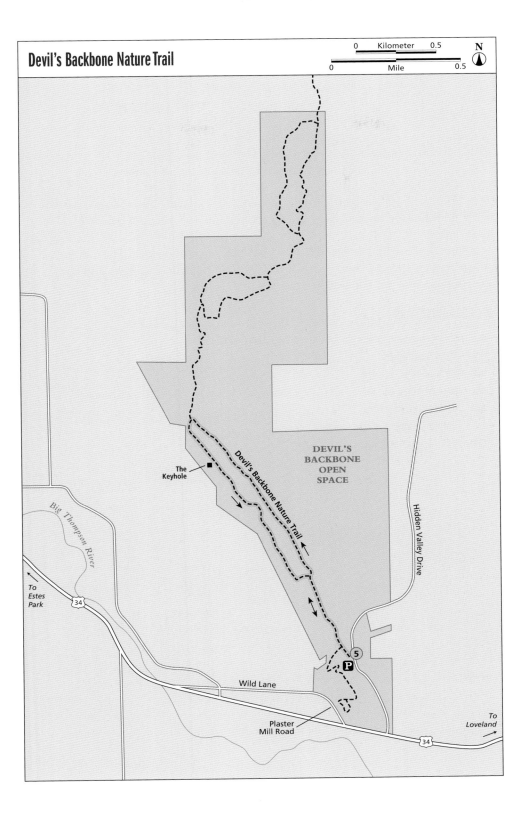

Devil's Backbone Nature Trail

DEVIL'S
BACKBONE
OPEN
SPACE

Devil's Backbone Nature Trail

The Keyhole

Big Thompson River

To Estes Park

34

Wild Lane

Plaster Mill Road

Hidden Valley Drive

5

P

To Loveland

34

Kilometer

Mile

N

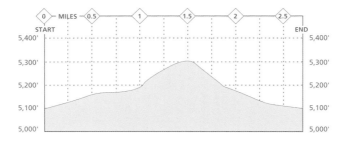

offers great views to the north, south, and east. Large yuccas line the trail and tall prairie grass fills the open hillsides as you continue in a southerly direction back to the trailhead.

At the 2-mile mark reach a metal post marked 3 and read the map. The trail makes a slight decline and you soon arrive at the first trail junction. Go right, and retrace your route back to the trailhead and the end of the hike.

Miles and Directions

0.0   Start by following the road toward the bed-and-breakfast.

0.3   Wood footbridges.

0.5   The trail forks; go right.

1.3   The trail forks; go left.

1.5   Arrive at the Keyhole.

2.2   Continue straight at trail junction.

2.7   Arrive back at the trailhead.

Estes Park/Lyons Area

6 Gem Lake Trail

A beautiful and accessible short hike into Rocky Mountain Park that leads to a small lake surrounded by unique granite rock.

Start: From the parking area, walk north to the start of the signed Gem Lake Trail.
Distance: 4.0 miles out and back
Hiking time: About 2 to 3 hours
Difficulty: Moderate
Trail surface: Steep and rocky in sections
Seasons: Year-round; can be snow packed in winter months

Other trail users: None
Canine compatibility: Dogs not permitted
Maps: Trails Illustrated Rocky Mountain National Park #200
Trail contact: Rocky Mountain National Park; (970) 586-1206

Finding the trailhead: From Estes Park, take Mac Gregor Avenue north for 0.8 mile, passing the Stanley Hotel. The road makes a hard right onto Mac Gregor Ranch, veer right on Devils Gulch Road (CR43) and continue 0.3 to Lumpy Ridge Road. Turn left on Lumpy Ridge Road and arrive at the trailhead at the dead end. GPS: N40 39.6486' / W105 51.3089'

The Hike

Start from the trailhead parking area and walk north on the signed Gem Lake Trail. Climb steeply arriving at the old Gem Lake/Twin Owls trail on the left. Go right into a beautiful pine, aspens and spruce forest. Reach a ridgeline and enjoy great views back to the west. The trail takes a small drop and crosses a small stream. Wild raspberries grow profusely in this area and are quite tasty when ripe in the summer months. The trail then climbs steeply up a series of switchbacks through quaking aspens and arrives at beautiful Gem Lake. Bring a lunch and enjoy the lake and its beautiful surroundings. Gem Lake is a popular trail and sees heavy traffic during the summer months. Arrive at the trailhead/parking area early and expect heavy foot traffic during the summer months.

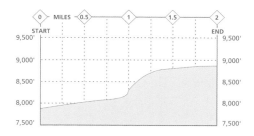

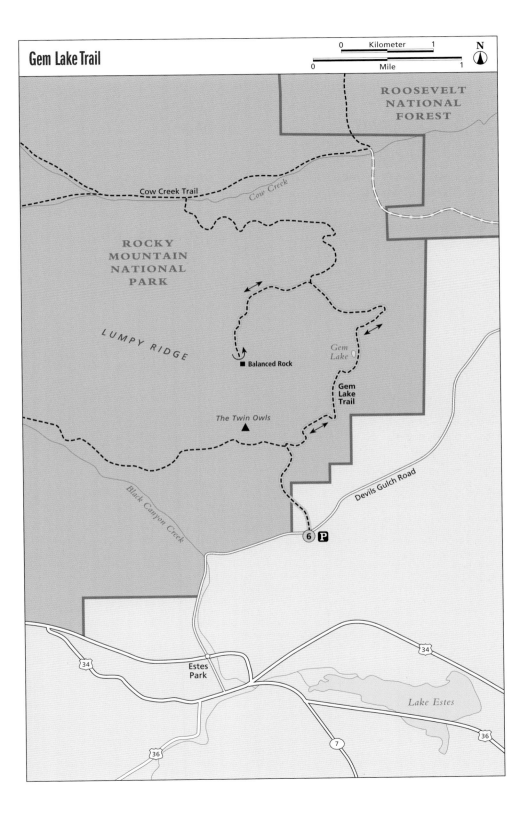

Gem Lake Trail

ROOSEVELT
NATIONAL
FOREST

Cow Creek Trail

Cow Creek

ROCKY
MOUNTAIN
NATIONAL
PARK

LUMPY RIDGE

Gem
Lake

■ Balanced Rock

**Gem
Lake
Trail**

The Twin Owls ▲

Black Canyon Creek

Devils Gulch Road

6 🅿

34

Estes
Park

34

Lake Estes

36

7

36

N

Option: You can easily extend your hike 3.6 miles (1.8 one way) to precipitous Balanced Rock. Skirt the lake on the left and then scramble through a tight passage in the rock walls and descend towards Cow Creek. Arrive at the Cow Creek and then follow the trail up to the rock. Retrace your route back to the Gem Lake.

Miles and Directions

0.0 Access the trailhead near the kiosk at the parking area.

0.5 Reach a trail junction with the old Gem Lake/Twin Owl Trail on the left. Go right.

1.2 Pass through beautiful aspens, spruce and pine forest.

2.0 Arrive at Gem Lake.

4.0 Arrive back at the trailhead.

7 Glacier Gorge

In my opinion this is the most beautiful spot in Rocky Mountain National Park. Spectacular scenery, beautiful wildflowers, cascading waterfalls, and beautiful alpine lakes are what you will find on your hike into Glacier Gorge. Bring along a fishing rod and a camera.

Start: From the parking area, cross the road and follow the signs for Alberta Falls.
Distance: 9.6 miles out and back
Hiking time: About 4 to 6 hours
Difficulty: Moderate to strenuous
Trail surface: Well-traveled and smooth on the first mile of the trail. The trail becomes quite rocky up to Black Lake.
Seasons: June to Oct

Other trail users: None
Canine compatibility: Dogs not permitted
Maps: Trails Illustrated Rocky Mountain National Park #200
Trail contact: Rocky Mountain National Park/USDA Forest Service; (970) 586-1206
Other: Camping is available in group campsites. A permit is required.

Finding the trailhead: From Estes Park, head west on US 36 past the Rocky Mountain National Park entrance station. Travel 0.3 mile past the ranger station and go left on Bear Lake Road. Follow Bear Lake Road for 8.5 miles to a parking area at a sharp hairpin turn. The hike starts here. GPS: N40 18.3888' / W105 38.2370'

The Hike

Cross the road from the parking area to reach the trailhead. Go left, following the sign for Alberta Falls. Cross a bridge and ignore a trail on the right. Continue straight and enjoy easy hiking through a forest of aspens, spruce, and lodgepole pines. Cross over several bridges and climb to Alberta Falls. Step to the left and enjoy the spectacular waterfall, which has cut an impressive gorge with its forceful waters. Alberta Falls is a mere 0.6 mile from the trailhead and can be extremely crowded. Don't worry, like most trails in the park, the farther away from the trailhead you get, the fewer people there are.

After the falls the trail begins a steady climb up several long switchbacks. Towering granite cliffs are off to the right and the views open up to the north, east, and west. At around the 1.4-mile mark you reach a junction with the North Longs Peak Trail on the left. Continue straight. Reach a high point and then follow the trail down a gentle grade through a scree slope, with Glacier Creek on the left. The tops of the towering rock walls of The Spearhead and Chiefhead peak can be seen in a commanding position at the western end of Glacier Gorge.

Drop down through the pines and reach a trail junction. The trail to Loch Vale goes to the right. Continue straight and down, crossing Icy Brook and then a log bridge over Glacier Creek. The trail goes right and follows granite steps up to where the path seems to disappear. Don't panic. Follow cairns up through granite slick rock to Mills Lake and spectacular views of Glacier Gorge.

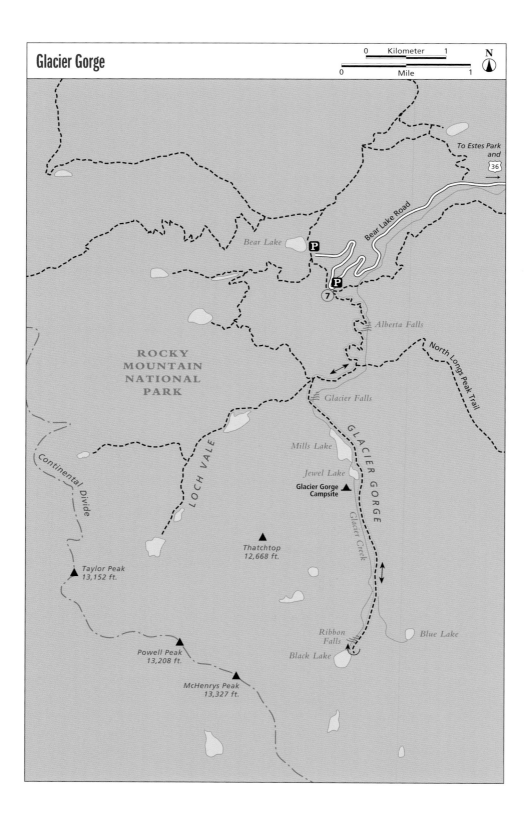

Glacier Gorge

0 Kilometer 1
0 Mile 1

N

To Estes Park and
36 →

Bear Lake Road

P

Bear Lake

P

7

Alberta Falls

ROCKY
MOUNTAIN
NATIONAL
PARK

North Longs Peak Trail

Glacier Falls

GLACIER GORGE

Mills Lake

LOCH VALE

Jewel Lake

Glacier Gorge
Campsite

Glacier Creek

Continental Divide

Thatchtop
12,668 ft.

Taylor Peak
13,152 ft.

Ribbon
Falls

Blue Lake

Black Lake

Powell Peak
13,208 ft.

McHenrys Peak
13,327 ft.

Take a break on one of the many rocks near the shoreline of this spectacular alpine lake. Mills Lake is extremely popular with anglers, and for some hikers is a destination in itself. To continue, the trail goes a little left, into the pines,

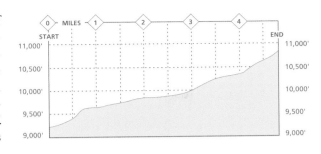

and avoids the moist areas around the shoreline of Mills Lake. Travel through the pines and reach Jewel Lake.

Jewel Lake sits in an open area surrounded by thick bog grasses and alpine wildflowers. The trail stays left of the lake and travels across several wood boardwalks through the moist area around the lake. Enjoy the wildflowers that grow profusely in the rich, fertile soil.

After crossing the boardwalks the trail stays close to Glacier Creek; use boulders to avoid getting your feet wet. Wildflowers bloom everywhere and light up the trail with their brilliant colors. At around the 3.5-mile mark, arrive at a trail junction at a bridge. The Glacier Gorge Campsite lies to the right, over the stream. Continue straight and up, using stone stairs to negotiate a steep section past a small waterfall. The trail goes left up a talus slope away from the stream, following rock cairns up to a level area near Black Lake.

Skirt the lake on the left, using a rock shelf to access the trail on the other side. Climb up and down, and reach a beautiful open area near the west end of Black Lake. This cirque is absolutely beautiful and can't be described with my meager writing skills. Ribbon Falls lies up and to the right, as do the towering, rocky summits of Arrowhead and McHenrys peaks.

Straight ahead lie the impressive vertical rock summits of The Spearhead and Chiefhead peak, dominating the western skyline. Hopefully you brought a camera, and if you brought a lunch, this is the spot to eat it. A climber's trail goes up to the left, along a creek, and gains a flat area filled with small tarns and bogs. Feel free to explore if you have the time or energy. This hike ends at Black Lake. Retrace your route back to the trailhead.

Miles and Directions

0.0 Start by crossing the road to the trailhead.

0.6 Reach Alberta Falls.

1.9 Trail to Loch Vale goes right. Continue straight on the Glacier Gorge Trail.

2.5 Arrive at Mills Lake.

3.5 Pass the Glacier Gorge Campsite.

4.8 Arrive at Black Lake.

9.6 Arrive back at the trailhead.

8 Estes Cone

Incredible views, an abandoned mine, and beautiful hiking on a well-maintained trail are the main attractions on this great hike up to the symmetrical summit of Estes Cone. One of the best short hikes in Rocky Mountain National Park.

Start: From the parking area, access the marked Longs Peak Trail.
Distance: 6.4 miles out and back
Hiking time: About 4 to 6 hours
Difficulty: Moderate to strenuous. The last grunt up to the summit is quite steep and strenuous.
Trail surface: Well-traveled and smooth on the first mile of the trail. The upper section is rocky and the trail all but disappears near the rocky summit of Estes Cone.

Seasons: May to Nov
Other trail users: Equestrians
Canine compatibility: Dogs not permitted
Maps: Trails Illustrated Rocky Mountain National Park #200
Trail contact: Rocky Mountain National Park/ USDA Forest Service; (970) 586-1206
Other: Camping is available at the trailhead and at Moore Park

Finding the trailhead: From Boulder, take US 36 north to the town of Lyons. Turn left on CO 7 and travel 22 miles. Turn left at a sign for the Longs Peak Trailhead. Go 1 mile to the Longs Peak Trailhead, campground, ranger station, and parking area. GPS: N40 17.4303' / W105 34.0207'

The Hike

This hike starts at the very popular Longs Peak Trailhead. The trailhead is extremely busy during the summer months, and it is difficult to secure a parking spot during this time. Arrive early or do the hike during the week to increase your chances of getting a parking spot.

The start of the hike follows the Longs Peak Trail up through a dense coniferous forest on a well-maintained trail. The trail climbs to a junction with the Storm Pass Trail at around the 0.5-mile mark, and the Estes Cone comes into view. Go right at the trail junction, Storm Pass Trail, following the trail into a mixed forest of aspens and pines. The trail climbs, descends, and traverses below Pine Ridge; at the 1.4-mile mark the trail crosses over Inn Brook via a wood footbridge, and reaches the Eugenia Mine site. All that is left of the old mine are an old, rusted boiler, tailings, and logs from the Norwall cabin. Carl P. Norwall worked the mine in the early 1900s, but soon left the area because all his work proved to be fruitless.

Skirt the cabin on the right and drop down through a dense forest of lodgepole pines to a small, open meadow. The meadow is quite lush, and during the summer months wildflowers grow profusely in this open area.

At around the 1.8-mile mark are a number of campsites. The Moore Park Campsite is in a pleasing setting along the edge of the meadow and offers a beautiful place to stop and spend the night.

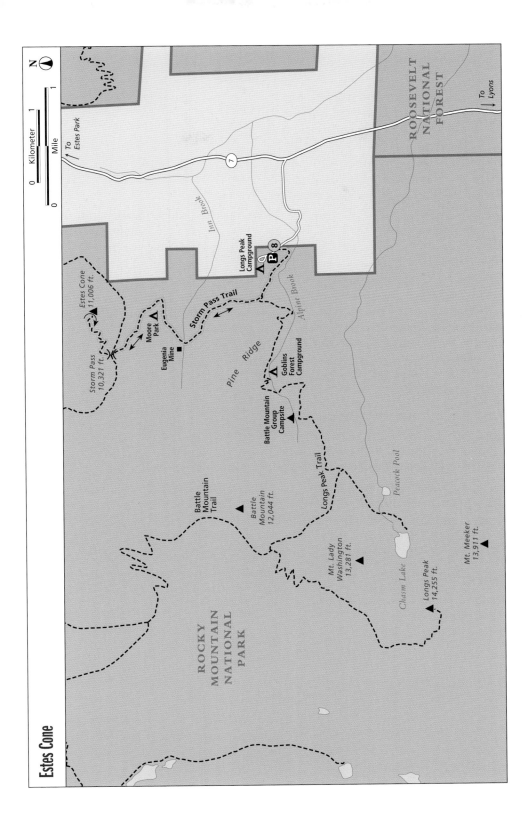

Estes Cone

Beyond the campsite you arrive at the 2-mile mark and a trail junction. Going right takes you to private property. Make a sharp left at Storm Pass Trail and begin climbing up a steep, forested slope to Storm Pass. The trail climbs steeply between rocks and wooden log stairs, with stunning views of the east face of Longs Peak on the left and the Estes Cone straight ahead.

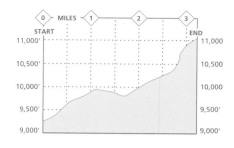

At 2.5 miles you reach the pass. Storm Pass is marked with trail signs and a large rock cairn. Take a short break here before the final grunt to the summit. The Storm Pass Cutoff Trail on the right was new as of 2001, and goes down to the Lily Lake Trailhead. Follow the Estes Cone Trail up through the limber pines, with the Estes Cone summit looming straight ahead. Enjoy the views, which become more spectacular the higher you climb.

Once out of the trees the trail climbs up through the rocks, following small rock cairns that guide you through the rock walls. Reach a small flat area, then head up and right to the true summit of the Estes Cone. Relax on the summit and enjoy spectacular views in all directions. Retrace your route back to the trailhead.

Miles and Directions

0.0   Start at the Longs Peak Trailhead.

0.5   The trail forks. Go right on the Storm Pass Trail.

1.4   Arrive at Eugenia Mine site and Inn Brook.

1.8   Arrive at the lovely Moore Park Campsite.

2.0   Continue straight at Trail junction.

2.5   Arrive at Storm Pass.

3.2   Arrive at summit of Estes Cone.

6.4   Arrive back at the trailhead.

9 Chasm Lake

Chasm Lake lies nestled in a rocky alpine cirque below the towering summits of Longs Peak (14,255 feet) and Mount Meeker (13,911 feet), the two highest summits in Rocky Mountain National Park. The cirque is absolutely stunning and is one of the most beautiful spots in all of Colorado. Do this hike!

Start: From the parking area, access the signed Longs Peak Trail.
Distance: 8.4 miles out and back
Hiking time: About 4 to 6 hours
Difficulty: Moderate to strenuous
Trail surface: Well-traveled and smooth for the first mile. The trail becomes quite rocky the closer you get to the lake.
Seasons: June to Oct

Other trail users: None
Canine compatibility: Dogs not permitted
Maps: Trails Illustrated Rocky Mountain National Park #200
Trail contact: Rocky Mountain National Park/ USDA Forest Service; (970) 586-1206
Other: Camping is available at the trailhead and at group campsites. A permit is required.

Finding the trailhead: From Boulder, take US 36 north to the town of Lyons. Turn left on CO 7 and travel 22 miles. Turn left at a sign for the Longs Peak Trailhead. Go 1 mile to the Longs Peak Trailhead, campground, ranger station, and parking area. GPS: N40 16.1843' / W105 33.2372'

The Hike

This hike starts at the very popular Longs Peak Trailhead. The trailhead is extremely busy during the summer months, and it is difficult to secure a parking spot during this time. Having hiked this trail at least fifteen times for climbing trips to the east face of Longs Peak, I recommend that you arrive early or do the hike during the week to increase your chances of getting a parking spot.

The hike follows the Longs Peak Trail up through a dense coniferous forest on a well-maintained trail. It then climbs up to the junction with the Storm Pass Trail. At 0.5 mile come to the trail junction, continue straight on the Longs Peak Trail and travel across Pine Ridge up to Alpine Brook. At around the 1-mile mark, Alpine Brook can be seen and heard on the left of the trail. Switchback up, with views to the east of the double peaks, aptly named Twin Sisters.

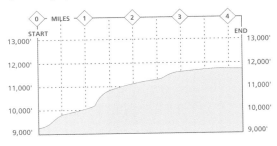

Longs Peak

At around the 1.3-mile mark, pass the Goblins Forest Campground on the left. The sheer rock wall of the east face of Longs Peak comes into view for the first time. It is quite impressive! The trail stays to the right of Alpine Brook and travels through a small scree garden up to Larkspur Creek. Things start to get serious from here on.

Cross over Larkspur Creek and begin a steep climb up several switchbacks to Alpine Brook. At Alpine Brook take a break and look around at the beautiful alpine flowers that grow in the moist soil around the banks of the creek. What a beautiful spot!

Chasm Lake

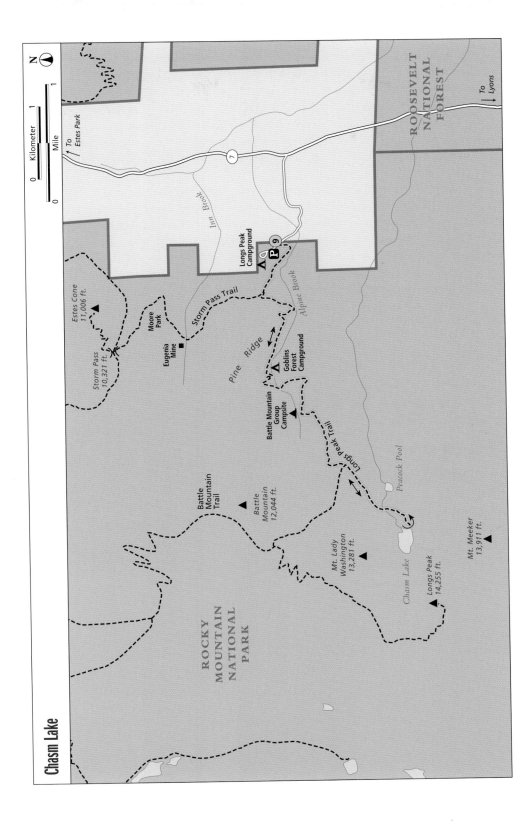

Time to move on. The trail now travels into Mill Moraine and up to timberline. Stunted flag trees dot the landscape and seem to be hanging on for dear life. The harsh conditions at this altitude make normal growth all but impossible for these hardy trees with branches on one side.

Continue climbing steeply into patches of rugged alpine grasses and be on the lookout for tiny alpine flowers that somehow manage to blossom in harsh conditions. Most people start to feel the effects of the altitude at this point. Drink lots of water and pace yourself.

Krummholz begin to appear as you approach Battle Mountain Group Campsite on the right of the trail and across Alpine Brook. These low-lying trees cling to the ground to survive in what is almost winterlike weather year-round. The trees almost look like groundcover, but in spite of their appearance can live to be hundreds of years old.

The trail keeps climbing, and if you want to reach Chasm Lake, so do you. Keep moving; before you know it you reach a trail junction and a breathtaking view of the east face of Longs Peak. The trail to the right continues up into the boulder field and to the summit of Longs Peak. Continue straight on Longs Peak Trail and along the southern flank of Mount Lady Washington (13,281 feet). The trail climbs briefly, then makes a gradual descent to Chasm Lake. Off to the left are Peacock Pool and Columbine Falls.

Reach Chasm Meadows and enjoy the abundant wildflowers. Cross a small stream and travel past the ranger's rescue cabin. Climb up through the rocks and voila; arrive at beautiful Chasm Lake. Take a break, then retrace your steps to the trailhead.

Miles and Directions

0.0   Start by following the Longs Peak Trail.

0.5   The trail forks.

1.3   Goblins Forest Campground.

2.5   Battle Mountain Group Campsite.

3.8   Chasm Lake junction.

4.2   Reach Chasm Lake. Retrace your steps.

8.4   Arrive back at the trailhead.

10 Calypso Cascades

This is a great hike down into the Wild Basin area of Rocky Mountain National Park and to Calypso Cascades. Calypso Cascades is a beautiful, tumbling waterfall that drops more than 100 feet down a forested hillside. The falls are formed by the raging waters of North Saint Vrain Creek. The trails in Rocky Mountain National Park are well maintained and marked with accurate distances at most trail junctions.

Start: From the parking area, walk west to the signed Allenspark Trail.
Distance: 6.2 miles out and back
Hiking time: About 3 to 4 hours
Difficulty: Moderate
Trail surface: Well-traveled and smooth for the first mile of the trail. The trail becomes rocky and root-filled near Calypso Cascades.

Seasons: June to Oct
Other trail users: Equestrians
Canine compatibility: Dogs not permitted
Maps: Trails Illustrated Rocky Mountain National Park #200
Trail contact: Rocky Mountain National Park/ USDA Forest Service; (970) 586-1206

Finding the trailhead: From Boulder, take US 36 to the town of Lyons. Turn left on CO 7 and travel 17 miles to Allenspark. Turn left into Allenspark and make a right on CR 90 (at the post office). Travel 1.2 miles to a fork in the road. Bear left at the fork onto CR 90 and travel 1 mile to the Allenspark Trailhead on the left. Park here to start the hike. GPS: N40 11.5257' / W105 33.1055'

The Hike

From the trailhead, the trail makes a gentle climb through dense spruce forest to a small stream crossing. The trail up to this point is fairly smooth and free of rocks. Beyond the creek the trail climbs to a trail junction on rockier tread, still deep in the trees, with limited views to the north.

At the trail junction of Allenspark Trail and Finch Lake Trail you go left, following the sign to Finch Lake. The trail becomes extremely rocky and climbs a stair of stone, with good views of Mount Meeker and Longs Peak.

At the 1.8-mile mark you arrive at a three-way trail junction. Going right takes you to the Wild Basin Ranger Station, going left leads to Finch Lake, and straight ahead is your route to Calypso Cascades. The trail drops at a nice grade, with spruce trees and wildflowers hugging the trail. There are excellent views to the west, with Copeland Mountain (13,176 feet) dominating the skyline on the eastern side of the Continental Divide. To the north you can catch a glimpse of Mount Meeker (13,911 feet) and Longs Peak (14,255 feet), the highest point in Rocky Mountain National Park.

Remains of the 1978 Ouzel Fire are evident in this area, as many burned trees cover the steep slopes along the trail. The fire consumed more than a thousand acres

Calypso Cascades

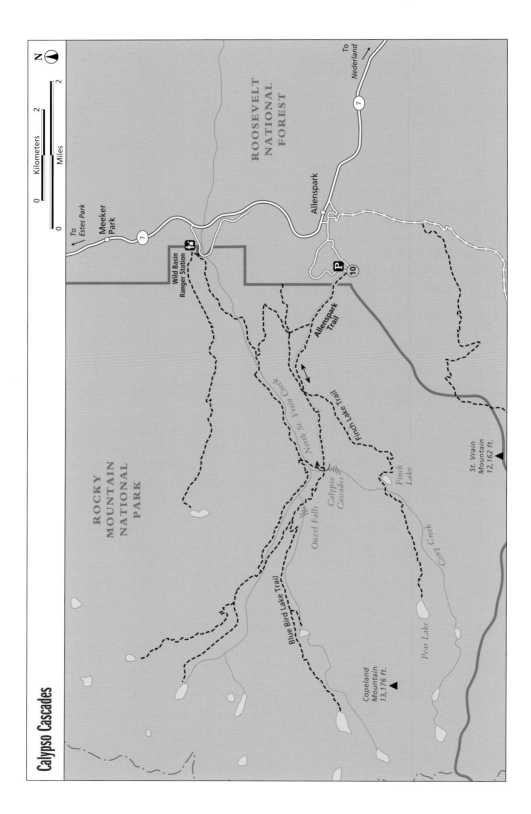

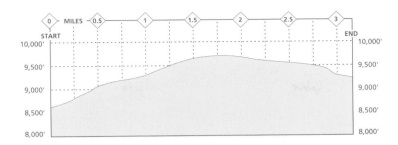

of prime forested land and almost took out the town of Allenspark before firefighters controlled the spreading flames. The fire also made the National Park Service review its policies on let-burn fires. Much regeneration has taken place since the fire, and the landscape is slowly returning to what it was before the mishap.

Continue down over a wood bridge across a drainage. The sound of the falls can be heard in the distance and becomes louder with every step you take down the trail. Be on the lookout for wildflowers along this section of the trail. Paintbrushes, columbines, and other colorful flowers line the hillsides, giving life to what just twenty-four years ago was a charred, barren landscape.

The trail becomes rocky as you near the falls, and it switchbacks down to two bridges that span the creek at a trail junction. The bridges are a great spot from which to view the falls and take pictures. The falls are named for the fairy slipper orchid (*Calypso bulbosa*), a rare flower that blooms along the falls and trail during late spring and early summer.

This area can be extremely crowded on the weekends during the summer months. If you want to extend your hike, follow the signs for Ouzel Falls, which are just under a mile away.

After enjoying the falls, retrace your route back to the Allenspark Trailhead.

Miles and Directions

0.0 Start by following the Allenspark Trail into a dense spruce tree forest.

0.5 Cross a small stream.

0.8 Arrive at a junction with the Finch Lake Trail.

1.8 Trail to Calypso Cascades and Ouzel Falls.

3.1 Calypso Cascades.

6.2 Arrive back at the trailhead.

11 Finch Lake

This is a great one- or two-day hike in the Wild Basin area of Rocky Mountain National Park. Wildflowers, great views, and a beautiful alpine lake are the rewards for your efforts in this southern section of Rocky Mountain National Park.

Start: From the parking area, walk west to the signed Allenspark Trail.
Distance: 8.2 miles out and back
Hiking time: About 5 to 6 hours or overnight
Difficulty: Moderate
Trail surface: Well-traveled and smooth for the first mile of the trail. After that expect very rocky and root-filled tread all the way to Finch Lake.
Seasons: June to Oct

Other trail users: Equestrians
Canine compatibility: Dogs not permitted
Maps: Trails Illustrated Rocky Mountain National Park #200
Trail contact: Rocky Mountain National Park/ USDA Forest Service; (970) 586-1206
Other: Camping is available at Finch Lake. You must have a permit. Contact Rocky Mountain National Park headquarters to secure a camping permit.

Finding the trailhead: From Boulder, take US 36 to the town of Lyons. Turn left on CO 7 and travel 17 miles to Allenspark. Turn left into Allenspark and make a right on CR 90 (at the post office). Travel 1.2 miles to a fork in the road. Bear left at the fork and travel 1 mile to the Allenspark Trailhead on the left. Park here to start the hike. GPS: N40 11.5257' / W105 33.1055'

The Hike

From the trailhead, the trail makes a gentle climb through dense spruce forest to a small stream crossing. The trail up to this point is fairly smooth and free of rocks. Beyond the creek, the trail climbs to a trail junction on rockier tread, still deep in the trees, with limited views to the north.

After 1.8 miles go left at the trail junction, following the sign to Finch Lake. The trail becomes extremely rocky and climbs a stair of stone, with good views of Mount Meeker (13,911 feet) and Longs Peak (14,255 feet).

At the 1.8-mile mark you arrive at a trail junction. Going right takes you to the Wild Basin Ranger Station; straight ahead and a little over a mile away is Calypso Cascades. For this hike you go up and left, following the Finch Lake Trail.

The trail climbs at a gentle grade into the remnants of 1978 Ouzel Fire. The fire consumed more than a thousand acres of

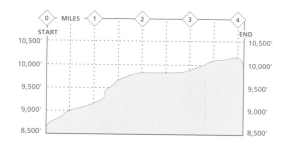

Finch Lake

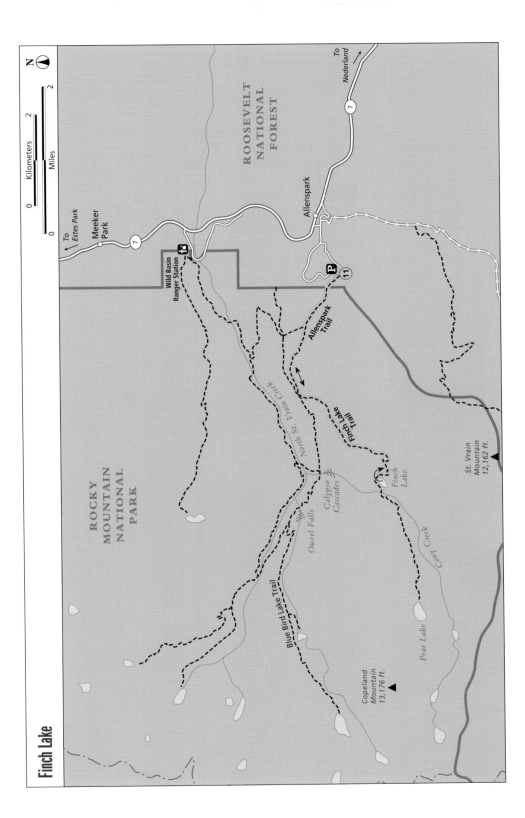

timber and left a huge black scar on the surrounding landscape. The trail cuts right through a large stand of charred trees and is quite spooky-looking. Looking around, you will notice how the forest has begun to rejuvenate itself, with batches of blueberry bushes, small stands of aspen and pine trees, and beautiful wildflowers growing. The most common flowers along this section of the trail are the narrowleaf puccoon, alpine daisy, and my favorite wildflower, the elephantella. There are great views through the dead trees to the north and west, with snow-covered peaks dotting the skyline.

The rocky trail stays fairly level as you work your way through a forest of moss-draped pines to a small bridge over North Saint Vrain Creek. This stretch of trail has been well maintained, with trail builders working to remove rocks, trees, and other debris, and installing small bridges over wet areas, making travel through this section much easier. Hats off to these folks for all their hard work.

Once past the bridge the trail drops down steeply on very rocky tread to your destination, Finch Lake. A sign will point you to campsites if you are staying overnight. The lake is stocked with cutthroat trout, so bring a fishing rod and enjoy an afternoon of great fishing in a beautiful setting. If you plan on spending the night, a written permit from Rocky Mountain National Park is required.

For the return trip, retrace your route back to the trailhead.

Miles and Directions

- **0.0** Start from the parking area and access the signed Allenspark Trail.
- **0.5** Reach a small stream crossing.
- **0.8** Arrive at a trail junction and continue straight.
- **1.8** Trail to Ouzel Falls goes right.
- **2.2** Remnants of the old Ouzel Fire.
- **3.5** Small bridge over North Saint Vrain Creek.
- **4.1** Arrive at beautiful Finch Lake.
- **8.2** Arrive back at the trailhead.

12 Lion Gulch Trail

A beautiful hike up through Lion Gulch brings you to Homestead Meadow, the site of numerous, abandoned settlements from the late 1800s and early 1900s.

Start: Cross over the bridge and travel through a small meadow into the trees on the signed Lion Gulch Trail 949.
Distance: 5.6 miles out and back
Hiking time: About 2 to 3.5 hours
Difficulty: Moderate
Trail surface: Mostly smooth with rocky sections
Seasons: Spring, summer, and fall
Other trail users: Equestrians

Canine compatibility: Dogs permitted
Maps: Trails Illustrated Cache la Poudre-Big Thompson #101
Trail contact: Arapaho and Roosevelt National Forests and Pawnee National Grassland; (970) 295-6600
Other: Camping is available along the trail and at Homestead Meadow.

Finding the trailhead: From Boulder, follow US 36 to the town of Lyons. Travel through Lyons, and then drive an additional 12.2 miles on US 36 toward Estes Park, to the Lion Gulch Trailhead on the left. Parking and a restroom are available here. GPS: N40 18.5390' / W105 24.1866'

The Hike

From the parking area, pass the restroom on the right and go down to the first footbridge. Cross over the bridge and travel through a small meadow into the trees and up to the second footbridge. Cross the footbridge; on the other side the trail forks. The track to the right is for horses and to the left is for hikers. Go left up the steep, rocky hill on rock and wood steps.

The trail climbs away from the creek on extremely rocky tread. Gain the ridge, with US 36 on the right. Drop again to the creek and through a small open meadow filled with pine and young aspen trees. Cross over a third footbridge and begin a short climb. The trail now travels through a dense forest of beautiful ponderosa pines, Douglas firs, and mature aspen trees. At one point the moss-covered trees create a canopy and the trail is cushioned with fragrant needles.

Make several stream crossings via log bridges, and at around the 1.7-mile mark begin a steep, narrow climb away from the creek. This trail is very popular with horseback riders. If you happen to meet riders, give the right of way and do not spook the horses. Certain sections of the trail are quite narrow, and spooking the horses could result in injury to horse and rider.

At around the 2-mile mark you cross the creek for the last time, with a small waterfall beside the trail. Continue climbing on the narrow trail, with granite rock formations on the right and numerous downed trees on the left. The trees must have fallen victim to some disease or beetle infestation. The rugged country surrounding

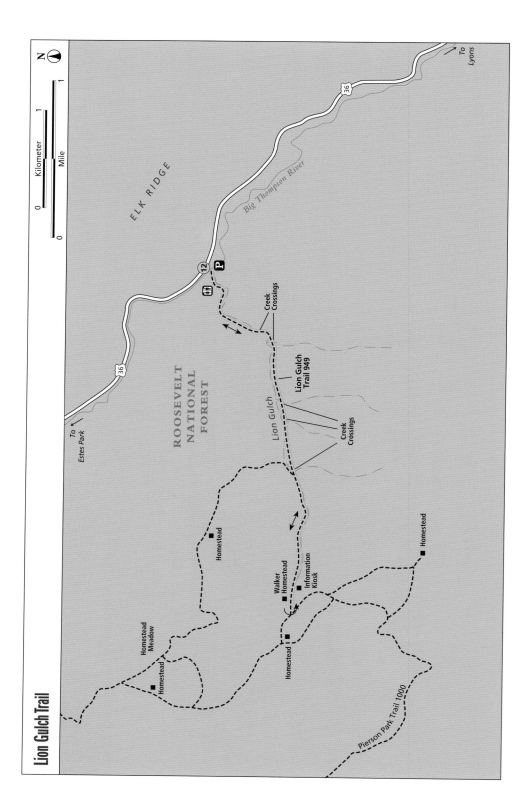

Lion Gulch Trail

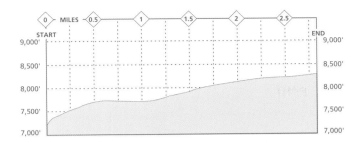

the trail is the perfect environment for mountain lions, and several of the big cats have been seen in the area.

At around the 2.3-mile mark, the trail follows what seems to be an old wagon road, and Homestead Meadow appears. Tall meadow grasses, wildflowers, and proud ponderosas surround the trail up to a kiosk. Be on the lookout for elk that graze on the meadow grasses.

At around the 2.6-mile mark arrive at the kiosk, which has information on the early settlers of the area. Read the information and continue up the trail past a water trough to a trail junction. At the 2.7-mile mark several trail markers give mileages to various homesteads. For this hike, continue straight up the open meadow to the Walker Homestead, on the right at the 2.8-mile mark.

Feel free to explore the many miles trails and the various homesteads in the area, or take a break and enjoy some lunch before heading back to the Lion Gulch Trailhead.

Miles and Directions

0.0   Start from the parking area; walk west to the signed Lions Gulch Trail.

0.3   Arrive at the first of three footbridges.

0.5   Arrive at the second footbridge.

0.9   Arrive at third footbridge.

2.0   Last of the creek crossings.

2.7   Homestead Meadow.

2.8   Arrive at historical Walker Homestead.

5.6   Arrive back at the trailhead.

13 Button Rock Preserve

Fishing, wildlife viewing, and exceptional hiking can be found in the Button Rock Preserve, and this hike will allow you the opportunity to experience all of these activities.

Start: From the parking area, walk north past the gate on a wide dirt road.
Distance: 5.9-mile loop
Hiking time: About 2 to 4 hours
Difficulty: Moderate
Trail surface: Lower section follows a smooth service road and the upper section travels through a short, rocky stretch

Seasons: Early spring to late autumn
Other trail users: Equestrians
Canine compatibility: Dogs must be on leash
Maps: USGS Boulder County City of Longmont/Button Rock Preserve map
Trail contact: City of Longmont; http://www.ci.longmont.co.us/openspace/index.htm

Finding the trailhead: From the town of Lyons, follow US 36 toward Estes Park for 3.8 miles to CR 80. Go left on CR 80 and travel 2.8 miles to a parking area and the start of the hike. GPS: N40 13.4220' / W105 20.3445'

The Hike

From the parking area follow the road up past a gate. Pass a handicapped-accessible trail on the left, and begin a gradual climb up the road, passing Longmont Reservoir on the right. Several rock walls on the right, at the spillway, are popular with rock climbers, and during the summer months you might see them clawing their way up the granite walls.

Continue up the service road, with North Saint Vrain Creek on the right, to the Sleepy Lion Trail on the left at about the 1.2-mile mark. This area is popular for fly-fishing and can be quite crowded during the summer months.

Go left on the Sleepy Lion Trail, into the trees and up Deadman Gulch. The trail now begins a steep climb on a smooth, narrow trail through thick stands of ponderosa pines and Douglas firs to a beautiful meadow. The trail winds back to the north, is easy to follow, and is quite pleasant, with views to the north.

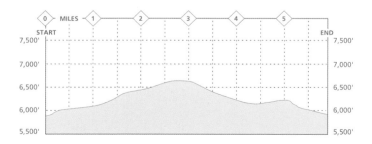

Button Rock Preserve

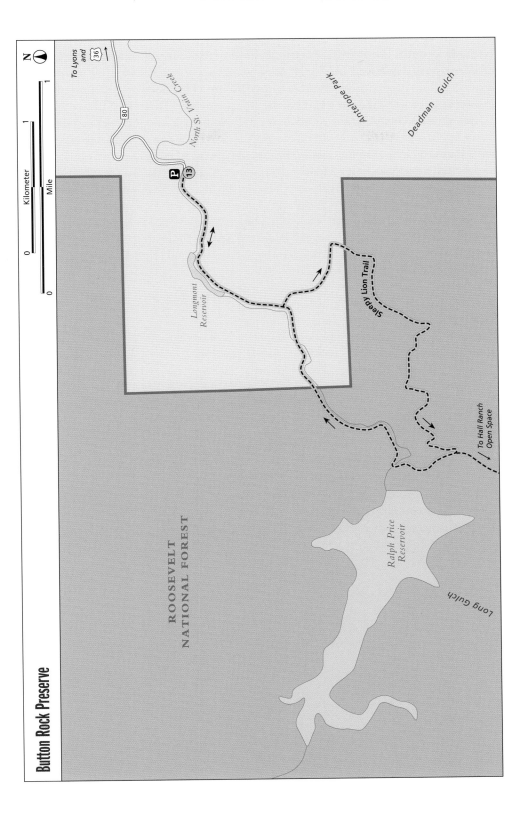

At around the 2-mile mark the trail leaves the forest and cuts across a beautiful, open meadow with great views of Rocky Mountain National Park. The meadow is quite picturesque, with wildflowers and yuccas growing along with tall meadow grasses. This is a good spot to take a break.

After traveling through the meadow the trail heads back into the trees and drops down into the ponderosa and pine trees. The elevation loss doesn't last long, and the trail begins to climb through and around several boulders, and follows an old fence line. Before long you reach a junction with a new trail that links Hall Ranch Open Space with the Sleepy Lion Trail. Continue on the Sleepy Lion Trail, with views to the north and the Ralph Price Reservoir.

Skirt past several large boulders, with open views to the north, and reach an old service road. Go right on the road and begin the descent to the spillway for the Price Reservoir. The road switchbacks down through the pines, and just before the spillway cuts through a narrow gulch filled with willows, aspens, and pines. Reach the service road and contour around the spillway, with its water shooting out forcefully into North Saint Vrain Creek. Follow the road down past a restroom and along the creek back to the parking area and the end of the hike.

The area is a wildlife preserve and is open to foot travel only. The City of Longmont built the Ralph Price Reservoir in the late 1960s; it is named for a former mayor. In the winter fishing is not allowed at the reservoir and at other times is allowed by permit only. Bald eagles roost and hunt along the shores of the reservoir, and bighorn sheep can be seen in the more remote areas above and around the dam.

Miles and Directions

0.0 Start from the parking area and walk north past a gate on a wide dirt road.

1.2 Arrive at Sleepy Lion Trail junction.

2.9 Arrive at a junction with the Hall Ranch Trail.

3.5 Arrive at the Ralph Price Reservoir.

5.9 Arrive back at the trailhead.

14 Hall Ranch

One of the best day hikes in the Estes Park/Lyons area. Beautiful vistas, stunning sandstone cliffs, abundant wildlife, cacti, and flower-filled meadows are what you are going to see on this hike. Pick up a Hall Ranch brochure from the kiosk and enhance your hike by reading the information in the brochure.

Start: From the parking area, walk past the kiosk to the signed Bitterbrush Trail.
Distance: 10.0-mile loop
Hiking time: About 2 to 4 hours
Difficulty: Moderate to strenuous
Trail surface: Ranges from very smooth to extremely rocky
Seasons: Year-round

Other trail users: Mountain bikers and equestrians
Canine compatibility: Dogs must be on leash or voice control
Maps: Boulder County Open Space/Hall Ranch map
Trail contact: Boulder County Open Space; (303) 678-6200

Finding the trailhead: From Boulder, travel west on US 36 to Lyons and the junction with CO 7. Go left on CO 7 for 1.3 miles to the Hall Ranch Open Space trailhead and parking on the right. GPS: N40 12.4208' / W105 17.1966'

The Hike

From the upper parking area, travel past the kiosk and restrooms to access the Bitterbrush Trail and the start of the hike. Follow the well-marked Bitterbrush Trail west. Looking north you'll see impressive sandstone bluffs overlooking the trail, evidence of the constant change the earth undergoes. These exposed cliffs are at the interface, where the Rocky Mountains meet the flat, open plains, and are the result of upheaval in the earth almost 1.5 billion years ago.

The trail curves around on the north side of a hill through an area of granite boulders, cacti, mahogany oak, and tall prairie grasses. Reach a service road at around the 0.8-mile mark and stay on the Bitterbrush Trail and drop into a narrow gulch. Past a rocky section the trail starts to climb to the north. Yuccas, cacti, and ponderosas line the trail as you start to gain altitude.

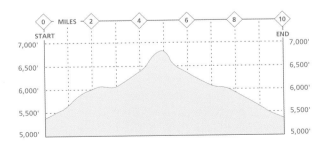

Sego Lily

Climb past several rocky sections (look on the ground for quartz crystals) and switchback up to a level area at the 2.1-mile mark. Take a break on the bench and admire panoramic views to the south, west, and east. Continue north past an interpretive sign; a large black-tailed prairie dog colony is in a large open meadow on the left. The trail makes a short drop and hugs the north side of the meadow, making a big sweep back to the west. Look for the deer and other wildlife that call this beautiful place home in the open meadow and tall grasses.

At around the 2.8-mile mark pass a second interpretive sign, and follow the trail into a beautiful stand of young ponderosa trees. Looming Mount Meeker (13,911 feet) and Longs Peak (14,258 feet) fill the western skyline. At around the 3.4-mile mark, look to the right and down into a rock-filled gully. Several large cliffs teeter on the hillside and are quite an impressive sight. At the 3.8-mile mark you arrive at a trail junction. Time to make a decision: do the Nelson Loop or turn back . . .

Let's do the Nelson Loop. Turn left on Nelson Loop Trail and travel into an open meadow, with great views to the south. Reach a bridge at the 4-mile mark and switchback up through the ponderosas to a beautiful, wide-open meadow. Take in the views to the west, and travel down to old Nelson Homestead on the right. Past the

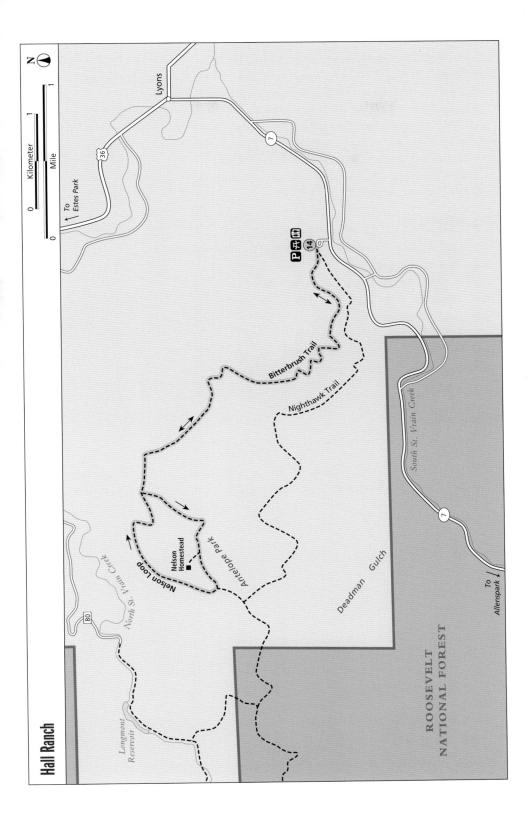

homestead the trail meets with the Nighthawk Trail on the left at the 4.9-mile mark. The Nighthawk Trail is 4.1 miles long and meets with the Sleepy Lion Trail at Button Rock Preserve. You remain on the Nelson Loop Trail.

The trail curves around the open meadow and heads back to the north. Reach a nice stand of ponderosas and follow the twisting trail back to the junction of the Nelson Loop and Bitterbrush Trail. From this point retrace your route back down the Bitterbrush Trail to the parking area and the trailhead.

This is a popular trail with mountain cyclists and equestrians. It is a multiuse trail so show common courtesy to all trail users.

Miles and Directions

0.0 Start by passing the restroom and picking up the Bitterbrush Trail.

0.8 Cross an old service road.

2.1 Reach the top of the hill and bench for resting.

3.8 Start of the Nelson Loop.

4.0 Cross over a foot bridge.

4.4 Remnants of an old homestead.

6.2 Arrive back at the junction with the Bitterbrush Trail.

10.0 Arrive back at the parking area/trailhead.

15 Rabbit Mountain

This fantastic hike offers expansive views of the northern foothills, east to the plains, and west to the Indians Peaks, Rocky Mountain National Park, and the Continental Divide. This hike takes you through stands of ponderosas and open meadows filled with cacti, yuccas, and wildflowers. Wildlife is abundant and can be seen year-round.

Start: From the parking area, visit the kiosk, grab a brochure, and take the Eagle Wind Trail east.
Distance: 4.1-mile loop
Hiking time: About 2 to 3 hours
Difficulty: Moderate
Trail surface: Rocky
Seasons: Year-round

Other trail users: Mountain bikers and equestrians
Canine compatibility: Dogs permitted
Maps: Boulder County Open Space/Rabbit Mountain map
Trail contact: Boulder County Open Space; (303) 678-6200

Finding the trailhead: From Boulder follow US 36 north to the town of Lyons. Turn east on CO 66 and travel 3 miles to North 53rd Street. Turn left on North 53rd Street and travel 3 miles to the trailhead and parking area. GPS: N40 14.4710' / W105 13.2606'

The Hike

From the parking area, visit the kiosk, grab a brochure, and take the Eagle Wind Trail east. The trail cuts across a hill on two switchbacks, travels through a burn area, and climbs to a junction with the Little Thompson Overlook Trail at the 0.5-mile mark.

Go right at the trail junction, across the service road, and head south on Little Thompson Overlook Trail. There are great views of the Flatirons to the south and Mount Meeker (13,911 feet) and Longs Peak (14,258 feet) to the west. At around the 0.9-mile mark, you reach a bench on the left side of the trail, facing west. This is a good spot to take a break and enjoy expansive views to the west and of the Continental Divide.

The trail continues south through an area of thick mahogany oak, pricklypear cacti, and tall prairie grasses to where the trail splits. Go right on Eagle Wind Trail and

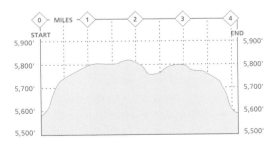

Horny Toad

soon enter into a stand of beautiful ponderosa pines. Lichen-covered rocks are scattered on and around the trail, along with yuccas and small cacti.

At around the 1.5-mile mark the trail cuts through a small open meadow and heads to the east. Rattlesnakes are common around Rabbit Mountain and like to warm themselves on sunny slopes and boulders. Use caution from mid-March to mid-October when hiking around Rabbit Mountain.

The trail makes a slight drop, then climbs a short hill back to the north, passing a wildlife-sensitive area on the right. There is no public access to the right of the trail, so respect the rules and obey the posted signs. The views to the north are beautiful and reveal sharp-cut ridges and steep-sloped hills. The trail reaches an old road at the 2.5-mile mark, and the hike follows the rocky road down and to the right through the ponderosas.

At around the 2.9-mile mark the trail bears to the right and in 0.2 mile you arrive back at a familiar trail junction with the Thompson Overlook Trail and the end of the loop. From this point retrace your route back to the trailhead.

Rabbit Mountain is a wonderful place to view wildlife. The abundance of prairie grasses and mahogany shrubs makes this area an important winter feeding ground for

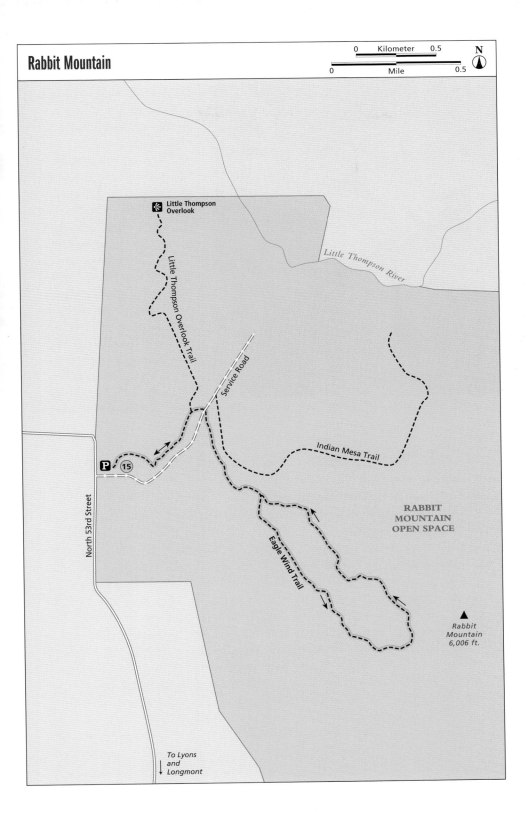

Rabbit Mountain

Little Thompson Overlook

Little Thompson River

Little Thompson Overlook Trail

Service Road

Indian Mesa Trail

P 15

North 53rd Street

RABBIT
MOUNTAIN
OPEN SPACE

Eagle Wind Trail

▲
Rabbit
Mountain
6,006 ft.

To Lyons
and
Longmont

0   Kilometer   0.5

0   Mile   0.5

N

both white-tailed and mule deer. In a rugged, rocky area like Rabbit Mountain, and with large herds of deer, more than likely you will find mountain lions, and it is no surprise that they have been spotted at Rabbit Mountain. The tall grasses and low-lying shrubs also provide feeding areas and homes for small rodents. In turn, the rodents attract high-flying raptors. There are also rattlesnakes, which are not aggressive, will not run you down, and for the most part want to be left alone. If you happen to see one of these beautiful reptiles, give the snake a lot of room and more than likely it will avoid you.

Sandstone Hogbacks near Rabbit Mountain

Miles and Directions

0.0 Start on the Eagle Wind Trail.

0.5 Junction with the Little Thompson Overlook Trail.

0.9 Pass a bench or better yet take a short break and enjoy the views.

1.0 The Eagle Wind Trail splits.

3.1 End of the Eagle Wind Trail Loop.

3.5 Go left, back toward the parking area.

4.1 Arrive back at the trailhead.

Boulder:
Foothills and Mountains

16 Ceran Saint Vrain Trail

A beautiful trail passes through lodgepole pines along South Saint Vrain Creek. This excellent family hike offers good campsites, fishing, and access. It's also a great spot for early summer wildflowers.

Start: From the trailhead, cross the bridge to access Ceran Saint Vrain Trail.
Distance: 6.2 miles out and back
Hiking time: About 2 to 4 hours
Difficulty: Strenuous
Trail surface: Smooth along the creek and rocky near Miller Rocks
Seasons: Early spring to late autumn
Other trail users: Mountain bikers and equestrians

Canine compatibility: Dogs must be on leash
Maps: Trails Illustrated Indian Peaks/Gold Hill #102
Trail contact: Boulder Ranger District, USDA Forest Service; (970) 295-6600; www .fs.usda.gov/contactus/arp/about-forest/ contactus
Other: Camping is available at the trailhead, along the creek, and near Miller Rocks.

Finding the trailhead: From the intersection of Broadway (CO 93) and Canyon (CO 119) in downtown Boulder, go north on Broadway for 4 miles to Lee Hill Road. Turn left, and follow Lee Hill Road to Old Stage Road. Follow Old Stage Road for 4 miles to Lefthand Canyon Road. Turn left on Lefthand Canyon Road and drive to Jamestown. Travel 4.7 miles past Jamestown to the turnoff for the trailhead. Go right into the parking area and trailhead. GPS: N39 54.0691' / W105 53.4029'

The Hike

The trailhead starts at a bridge over South Saint Vrain Creek, and guides you into a beautiful forest of lodgepole pines and wildflowers. This section of the trail is popular with campers and anglers, and can be very crowded on weekends during the summer months. The area near the trailhead, and the smooth water-worn rocks in the river are excellent spots to just hang out, eat some lunch, and enjoy the tumbling waters.

The trail climbs a short distance, then becomes narrow, with steep drop-offs to the right. Be on the lookout for wildflowers and clusters of beautiful fairy slipper orchids during the early summer months. (The fairy slipper is a rare flower of the orchid family that grows in the moist, shady evergreen forests of the Rocky Mountain foothills, and in

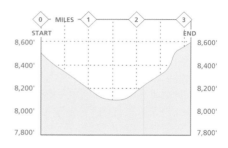

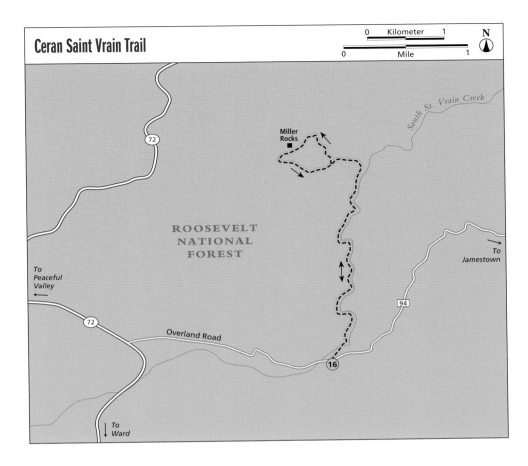

Ceran Saint Vrain Trail

0 Kilometer 1

0 Mile 1

N

Miller Rocks

South St. Vrain Creek

72

ROOSEVELT NATIONAL FOREST

To Jamestown

To Peaceful Valley

72

Overland Road

94

16

To Ward

the montane and subalpine ecosystems from Alaska in the north to New Mexico in the south.)

The trail pulls away from the river and makes a healthy descent to a trail junction at the 1.9-mile mark. Go left and up away from the river to a trail junction at the top of the hill. Go left again, up to another trail junction. The hike goes right on a narrow trail up to a junction with an old logging road. Go left and up the road to Miller Rocks on the right. There is a trail around the base of the rocks, and an easy scramble leads to the top of the rocks, revealing spectacular views west to the Indian Peaks.

Ceran Saint Vrain—guide, explorer, fur trader, and fort builder—played an important role in settling the wilderness now known as northern Colorado. With his partner, Charles Bent, he founded and built several forts in northern Colorado. Fort Saint Vrain, located at the confluence of the South Platte and Saint Vrain Rivers, is the most famous. He was active in politics, business, and military affairs, and his name will be forever intertwined with the early history and settlement of northern Colorado.

Miles and Directions

0.0 Start at the bridge over South Saint Vrain Creek.

1.9 Go left and up.

2.1 Trail junction at top of the hill. Go left and up.

2.4 Trail junction. Go right.

2.7 Go left.

3.1 Miller Rocks on the right.

6.2 Arrive back at the trailhead.

17 Mount Audubon

A wonderful day hike leads up to the beautiful alpine summit of Mount Audubon (13,223 feet). Wildflowers, panoramic high alpine views, and alpine lakes make this hike well worth the effort. This is a very strenuous hike with a lot of altitude gain in a long, 4-mile march to the summit. There are stunning views of Pawnee Peak, Mount Toll, Paiute Peak, Sawtooth Mountain, and Rocky Mountain National Park to the north. This is a very popular trail that sees a fair amount of traffic in the summer months. Your best bet to avoid the crowds would be to do the hike midweek.

Start: From the parking area, access the signed Beaver Creek Trail.
Distance: 8.0 miles out and back
Hiking time: About 4 to 6 hours
Difficulty: Strenuous
Trail surface: Well-traveled trail on the lower section, with very loose, rocky tread to the summit
Seasons: Late June to early Oct
Other trail users: None

Canine compatibility: Dogs must be on leash
Maps: Trails Illustrated Indian Peaks/Gold Hill #102
Trail contact: Boulder Ranger District, USDA Forest Service; (970) 295-6600; www .fs.usda.gov/contactus/arp/about-forest/contactus
Other: Camping is available at Brainard Lake Recreation Area.

Finding the trailhead: From the junction of CO 93 (Broadway) and CO 119 (Canyon) in downtown Boulder, go west on CO 119 for 18 miles to Nederland and the junction with CO 72. Go west on CO 72 for 10 miles to CR 102. Go left on CR 102 to the Brainard Lake Recreation Site and the Mitchell Creek Trailhead parking area. GPS: N40 04.5952' / W105 34.5231'

The Hike

The hike starts at the Beaver Creek Trailhead, located at the Mitchell Creek parking area above Brainard Lake. Access the well-marked Beaver Creek Trail on the north side of the parking area. The trail is well maintained and makes a gradual climb to a shelf and the Mount Audubon Trail. After about 0.5 mile of easy hiking through a dense spruce forest, the trail makes a sharp right turn up a steep switchback, with views out to the east.

At 1.3 miles the Beaver Creek Trail goes right down to Coney Flats Road. The Mount Audubon Trail continues straight. The trail takes a tight line up through a stand of twisted krummholz and a small boulder field. You are gaining considerable altitude at this point, as the pine trees disappear behind you. The trail cuts over a small, beautiful stream and up through a stunning alpine meadow to a snowfield.

At 2.5 miles the trail makes a sharp right away from a snowfield and climbs steeply through a boulder field to a broad, flat ridge with excellent views of the surrounding

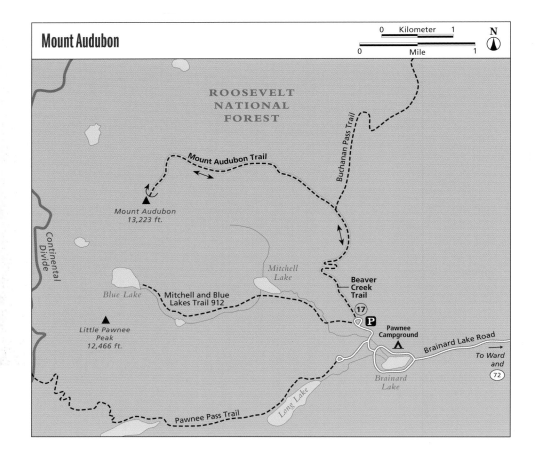

alpine peaks. At 3.5 miles the trail goes left, up a steep, rocky trail to the summit. There are a number of side trails that shoot off from the main trail and take a steep scramble to the summit. Follow the cairns and stay on the main trail. It is easier to gain the summit following the main trail, and less intrusive to the surrounding alpine environment. At 4 miles you arrive at the summit of Mount Audubon.

The last section of the hike lies above timberline and is exposed to violent lightning storms. Get an early start and try to be off the summit by noon during the thunderstorm season. The last mile of the trail gains 1,000 feet and can be very strenuous for those not acclimated to altitude. Take a break at one of the many rock shelters on the summit and enjoy the spectacular alpine scenery from this beautiful summit.

Nala, the Super Lab near the summit

C. C. Parry, a botanist, and zoologist J. W. Velie climbed the mountain in 1864 and named the peak after the famous naturalist, who never set foot in Colorado.

After you've summited, retrace your steps to the trailhead.

Miles and Directions

0.0 Start from the parking and access the signed Beaver Creek Trail.

0.4 The trail cuts right up a steep switchback.

1.3 Junction with the Beaver Creek Trail, continue straight on the Mount Audubon Trail 913.

1.9 Great views of the surrounding peaks and Blue Lake.

2.5 Steep switchbacks.

3.5 Climb steep switchbacks up to the summit.

4.0 Arrive on the Mount Audubon summit. Retrace your steps.

8.0 Arrive back at the trailhead.

18 Blue Lake

A wonderful day hike leads to Blue Lake in the Indian Peaks Wilderness Area. This short hike takes you up to a beautiful alpine lake surrounded by stunning alpine peaks.

Start: From the parking area, access the signed Mitchell Creek Trail.
Distance: 5.0 miles out and back
Hiking time: About 2.5 to 4 hours
Difficulty: Moderate
Trail surface: Well-traveled and rocky on the lower section, with loose, rocky, and wet conditions up to Blue Lake. Expect to find snow on the upper section of the trail well into June.
Seasons: June to Oct

Other trail users: Equestrians
Canine compatibility: Dogs must be on leash
Maps: Trails Illustrated Indian Peaks/Gold Hill #102
Trail contact: Boulder Ranger District, USDA Forest Service; (970) 295-6600; www .fs.usda.gov/contactus/arp/about-forest/ contactus
Other: Camping is available at Brainard Lake Recreation Area

Finding the trailhead: From the junction of CO 93 (Broadway) and CO 119 (Canyon) in Boulder, go west on CO 119 for 18 miles to Nederland and the junction with CO 72. Go west on CO 72 for 10 miles to CR 102. Go left on CR 102 to the Brainard Lake Recreation Site and the Mitchell Creek Trailhead parking area. GPS: N40 04.5952' / W105 34.5231'

The Hike

This is one of my favorite hikes in the Indian Peaks Wilderness Area, and you get a lot of bang for the buck on this hike. Beautiful views, spectacular wildflowers, lovely alpine lakes; this hike has it all. If you are planning to hike up to Blue Lake during the weekend in the summer months, arrive early to secure a parking space. The parking lot fills up quickly in summer and finding a space after early morning can be a problem.

The hike begins at the Mitchell Lake Trailhead, located near the restrooms at the Mitchell Lake Trailhead parking area. The Mitchell Lake Trail begins at an elevation of 10,472 feet and climbs to 11,352 feet (at Blue Lake) in just under 2.5

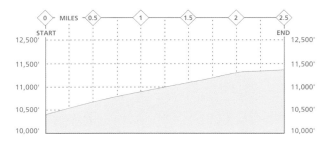

Laurel D'Antonio enjoying a beautiful summer day in the Indian Peaks

miles. The start of the trail is wide, level, and somewhat rocky. At the 0.2-mile mark you enter the boundary of the wilderness area, and the trail wanders through dense, tall spruce trees.

At around the 0.3-mile mark, cross over Mitchell Creek on a wood footbridge. After the footbridge the trail climbs gently to Mitchell Lake, with wildflowers and spectacular views of Mount Audubon (13,223 feet), Little Pawnee Peak, Mount Toll, and Paiute Peak. Mitchell Lake is a shallow, fourteen-acre lake that is stocked with cutthroat trout and is quite popular with anglers. The meadow around the lake is filled with wildflowers that grow profusely in the moist, fertile soil. Blanketflowers, alpine primrose, mountain lupines, mountain-avens, goldenbanner, and

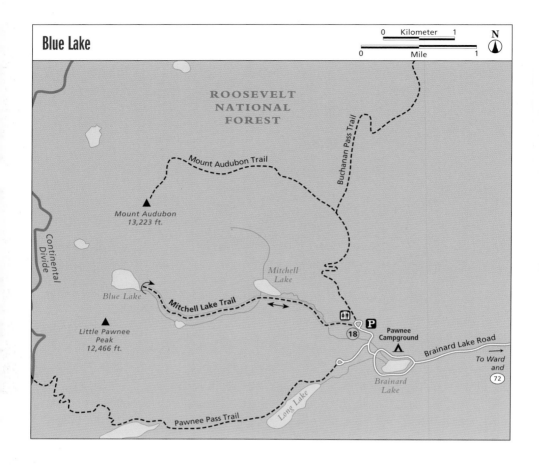

Blue Lake

ROOSEVELT NATIONAL FOREST

Buchanan Pass Trail

Mount Audubon Trail

Mount Audubon
13,223 ft.

Continental Divide

Mitchell Lake

Blue Lake

Mitchell Lake Trail

Little Pawnee
Peak
12,466 ft.

18

Pawnee
Campground

Brainard Lake Road

To Ward
and

72

Brainard
Lake

Long Lake

Pawnee Pass Trail

globeflowers are just a few of the flowers that blossom around Mitchell Creek and Mitchell Lake.

At the 1-mile mark the trail crosses over Mitchell Creek again, on a makeshift bridge of logs and fallen trees. After Mitchell Creek the trail climbs on log steps to a meadow with good views of the surrounding peaks. This is another place to stop and enjoy the views and the wildflowers. Wooden walkways guide you through the marshy area of the meadow and up to the drier, rocky section of the trail.

At around the 2-mile mark the trail cuts across a snowfield, following rock cairns, with Mitchell Creek and Little Pawnee Peak on the left. At the 2.5-mile mark, Blue Lake appears in a cirque below the towering summits of Mount Toll and Paiute Peak. Blue Lake covers almost twenty-three acres, is almost 100 feet deep, and is stocked with cutthroat trout.

Take a lunch break and enjoy the panoramic views and alpine splendor, then retrace your steps to the trailhead.

Summer in the Indian Peaks

Miles and Directions

0.0 Start on the Mitchell Lake Trail.

0.2 Arrive at the Indian Peaks Wilderness boundary.

0.8 Arrive at beautiful Mitchell Lake.

1.0 Cross over Mitchell Creek.

1.5 Alpine meadow and ponds.

2.5 Arrive at Blue Lake. Retrace your steps.

5.0 Arrive back at the trailhead.

19 Heart Lake

This spectacular hike climbs into a beautiful alpine basin, with the main attraction being Heart and Rogers Pass Lakes.

Start: From the parking area, cross the bridge to reach the start of the signed trail.
Distance: 8.4 miles out and back
Hiking time: About 4 to 6 hours
Difficulty: Moderate to strenuous
Trail surface: The lower section of the Heart Lake Trail has smooth tread and is wet in some spots. The upper section of the trail is wet, very rocky, and filled with roots and scattered downed trees.

Seasons: Early June to late Oct
Other trail users: Equestrians
Canine compatibility: Dogs must be on leash
Maps: Trails Illustrated Winter Park/Rollins Pass/Central City #103
Trail contact: Boulder Ranger District, USDA Forest Service; (970) 295-6600; www .fs.usda.gov/contactus/arp/about-forest/contactus
Other: Camping is available at Heart Lake

Finding the trailhead: From the junction of CO 93 (Broadway) and CO 119 (Canyon) in Boulder, go west on CO 119 for 18 miles to Nederland. Continue on CO 119 for 5 miles to Rollinsville and the junction with CR 149. Go right onto CR 149 for 7.5 miles to a fork in the road. Go left at the fork for 1 mile to East Portal, parking and the trailhead. GPS: N39 54.0691' / W105 53.4029'

The Hike

Heart and Rogers Pass Lakes are situated in an alpine valley below the jagged, rocky summits of Haystack Mountain and James Peak (13,249 feet). The trail to the lakes takes a direct line up a rocky and wet gulch along South Boulder Creek.

From the parking area, go left over South Boulder Creek, just before the Moffat Tunnel, to the trailhead and a kiosk. Follow the well-marked trail past the kiosk up along South Boulder Creek. The trail crosses three wood footbridges over Arapaho Creek, up to a meadow that has a pair of abandoned cabins in it. At the meadow there are three wood posts on the trail; to the right is the Forest Lakes Trail. You continue straight 0.8 mile to South Boulder Creek Trail 900 and begin a steep climb on rocky, root-filled, wet tread up a rock-infested gully.

The trail follows a line along the north side of South Boulder Creek in a dense, mature spruce forest. The spruce trees are draped with moss and the trail follows what was once a mining road.

At the 2.1-mile mark, the trail becomes level and angles left through an extremely wet section littered with beautiful wildflowers, then crosses South Boulder Creek. The trail is somewhat difficult to follow and uses an occasional wood plank to negotiate the wet sections. Because the trail becomes unclear through this

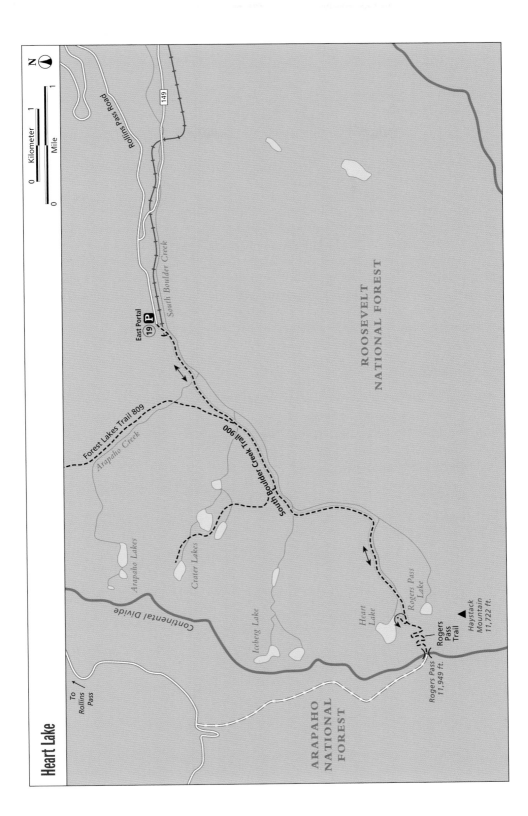

Heart Lake

N

0   Kilometer   1

0   Mile   1

To Rollins Pass

Continental Divide

ARAPAHO NATIONAL FOREST

Rollins Pass Road

149

East Portal

P

19

South Boulder Creek

Forest Lakes Trail 809

Arapaho Creek

Arapaho Lakes

Crater Lakes

Iceberg Lake

South Boulder Creek Trail 900

Heart Lake

Rogers Pass Lake

Rogers Pass Trail

Rogers Pass 11,949 ft.

Haystack Mountain 11,722 ft.

ROOSEVELT NATIONAL FOREST

section, stay near South Boulder Creek and look for red dots on the trees to lead you in the right direction.

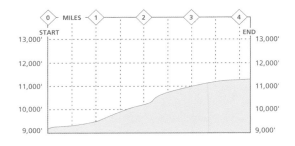

Past the wet section the trail becomes rocky and steep, as you gain altitude on your way up to Heart Lake. You are deep in a dense spruce forest along this stretch, but there is an occasional open area that reveals nice views of Nebraska Hill. I hiked this trail in early June, and the upper section of the trail still had a fair amount of snow on it, which made route-finding somewhat difficult.

At around the 3.8-mile mark, the trail comes out of the trees into a beautiful alpine basin, with Haystack Mountain and James Peak on the left. Reach a fork in the trail and go right to Heart Lake. Going to the left will take you to Rogers Pass Lake, Rogers Pass Trail, and the Continental Divide. I recommend camping at Heart Lake and spending at least two days exploring this beautiful and remote area.

After your visit, retrace your steps to the trailhead.

Miles and Directions

0.0 Start by crossing South Boulder Creek to the signed trailhead and kiosk.

0.4 Arapaho Creek goes off to the right.

0.8 Trail goes right to Forest Lakes; continue straight on South Boulder Creek Trail 900.

2.1 Cross over South Boulder Creek.

4.2 Arrive at Heart Lake. Retrace your steps.

8.4 Arrive back at the trailhead.

20 Heil Valley Ranch/Lichen Loop

This great family hike is in Boulder County's newest open space area. It is a great way to get the kids out into the woods on a short, scenic loop through stands of beautiful ponderosas and open meadows. Heil Valley Ranch is an excellent spot for wildlife viewing.

Start: From the parking area, walk east to the signed Lichen Loop Trail.
Distance: 1.3-mile loop
Hiking time: About 1 to 2 hours
Difficulty: Easy
Trail surface: Smooth and well maintained by volunteers and open space rangers
Seasons: Year-round

Other trail users: Equestrians
Canine compatibility: Dogs must be on leash or voice control
Maps: Boulder County Open Space/Heil Valley Ranch map
Trail contact: Boulder County Open Space; (303) 678-6200; www.bouldercounty .org/government/dept/pages/pos.aspx

Finding the trailhead: From Boulder, follow US 36 north toward the town of Lyons to Lefthand Canyon Road. Go left on Lefthand Canyon Road for 0.5 mile to Geer Canyon Road. Go right on Geer Canyon Road for 1.3 miles to the signed trailhead and parking area. GPS: N40 08.5700' / W105 18.0155'

The Hike

From the trailhead/picnic area, pass the information kiosk and follow the signs for the Lichen Loop. The trail goes over a wood bridge and heads left, up to the start of the loop portion of the hike.

Travel through stands of beautiful ponderosas and a meadow filled with tall grasses, yuccas, and cacti. Views to the north up the valley are spectacular, with sharp-cut canyons and open meadows. Reach a trail junction at around the 0.5-mile mark and go right, switchbacking up through the ponderosas. Past several large lichen-covered boulders, the trail breaks out into an open meadow with tall prairie grass and the occasional ponderosa tree. Views open to the south and east at upturned sedimentary rock along a ridgeline. The trail cuts through the open meadow and begins a gentle descent back toward the trailhead.

Enjoy the pleasant hiking through the meadow, close the loop, and retrace your steps back at the trailhead. Picnic tables are located near the trailhead, so bring a lunch and enjoy spending an afternoon with the family at this beautiful open space area.

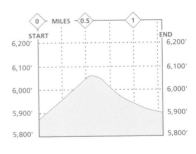

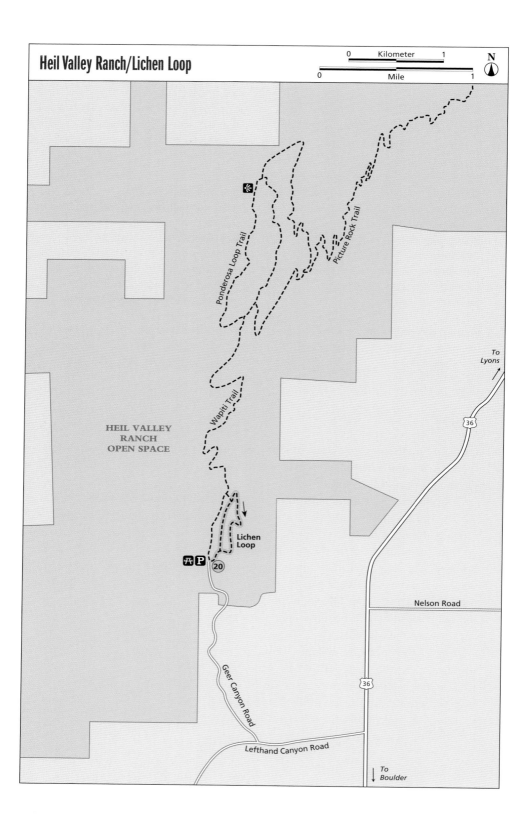

Miles and Directions

0.0   Start by passing the information kiosk and picking up the Lichen Loop.

0.5   Arrive at a trail junction.

1.3   Arrive back at the trailhead.

21 Heil Valley Ranch

One of Boulder's best hikes, this beautiful loop leads high into the foothills, passing through dense stands of ponderosa pines, open meadows with tall prairie grasses and spring wildflowers, and offers dramatic views north to Mount Meeker (13,911 feet) and Longs Peak (14,255 feet).

Start: From the parking area, walk north to the signed Wapiti Trail.
Distance: 8.1-mile loop
Hiking time: About 2.5 to 4 hours
Difficulty: Moderate
Trail surface: Smooth for the most part and is well maintained by volunteers and open space rangers
Seasons: Year-round

Other trail users: Mountain bikers and equestrians
Canine compatibility: Dogs must be on leash or voice control
Maps: Boulder County Open Space/Heil Valley Ranch map
Trail contact: Boulder County Open Space; (303) 678-6200; www.bouldercounty .org/government/dept/pages/pos.aspx

Finding the trailhead: From Boulder, follow US 36 north toward the town of Lyons to Lefthand Canyon Road. Go left on Lefthand Canyon Road for 0.5 mile to Geer Canyon Road. Go right on Geer Canyon Road for 1.3 miles to the signed trailhead and parking area. GPS: N40 08.5700' / W105 18.0155'

The Hike

From the trailhead/picnic area, pass the kiosk and follow the sign for the Wapiti Trail. Go left, up the short hill, and reach a service road. Follow the road north, with excellent views to the north and east.

At around the 0.5-mile mark you reach a gate and a spur to the Lichen Loop. Go left on the Wapiti Trail, through an open meadow filled with prairie dog mounds. Cross over a bridge and switchback up to an open meadow with open views to the south. Tall prairie grasses are mixed with yuccas, paintbrushes, and cacti.

The trail soon enters a dense ponderosa forest and climbs up to a service road. At around the 1.4-mile mark, the trail crosses a service road and climbs up through the trees to the remnants of an old stone building. The trail goes left at the ruins and continues to climb through ponderosas to a junction with the Ponderosa Loop Trail at the 2.7-mile mark. This is a nice spot to take a short break.

Go right on the Ponderosa Loop Trail and drop slightly to an open meadow with great views to the north and east. Enjoy open hiking with a southwest exposure. The trail goes back into the ponderosas, much shorter here than on the lower part of the trail, and climbs to a service road.

At the service road and the 3.5-mile mark, cross the road and wind back to the north, still on the Ponderosa Loop, and up toward an overlook. Reach the overlook

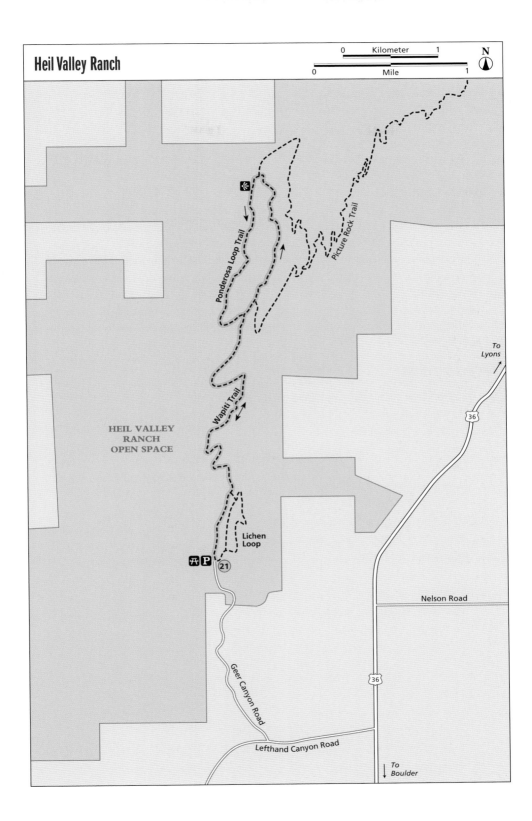

at the 3.9-mile mark, and enjoy the dramatic views west to Mount Meeker and Longs Peak, north to Saint Vrain Canyon, and east to the open plains. If you packed a lunch, this is the place to stop and eat it. Two benches at the overlook provide a comfortable spot to enjoy lunch and the views.

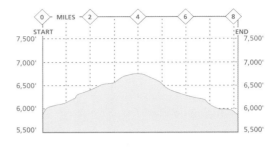

Past the overlook, the trail becomes a little rockier and climbs at a gentle grade up to a service road. Cross the road and at around the 4.3-mile mark reach a flat area with an amazing view west to Mount Meeker and Longs Peak, at 14,255 feet the highest point in Rocky Mountain National Park. Pass through a section of young ponderosas in a small meadow. The trail now begins to drop back down to the Wapiti Trail.

Reach the Wapiti Trail at around the 5.4-mile mark, closing the loop portion of the hike. Retrace your route back to the trailhead, with great views to the south and east.

Miles and Directions

0.0   Start from the parking area and access the signed Wapiti Trail.

0.5   The Wapiti Trail goes left.

0.7   Cross over a small wooden bridge.

1.4   Cross an old service road.

1.8   Arrive at the remnants of a homestead.

2.7   Arrive at the Ponderosa Loop Trail.

3.5   Cross an old service road.

3.9   Arrive at an overlook and spectacular views.

5.4   Arrive back at the Wapiti Trail, closing the loop.

8.1   Arrive back at the trailhead.

22 Mount Sanitas

This short hike leads up the Sanitas Valley to the summit of Mount Sanitas (6,863 feet). Once on top of Mount Sanitas you are rewarded with some of the best views to be had in Boulder County. Wildflowers, wildlife, strange rock formations, plus a true summit make for a must-do hike in the Boulder area.

Start: From the parking area, skirt the day-use pavilion and head right to the Sanitas Valley Trail, a wide dirt road.
Distance: 3.2-mile loop
Hiking time: About 1 to 2 hours
Difficulty: Easy to moderate
Trail surface: Smooth on the way up the valley, and becomes rocky to the summit and back down to the trailhead

Seasons: Year-round. Can be snowy and icy on the north-facing slopes in the winter.
Other trail users: Equestrians
Canine compatibility: Dogs must be on leash or voice control
Maps: USGS Boulder County, Boulder County Open Space/Mount Sanitas map
Trail contact: City of Boulder Mountain Parks and Open Space

Finding the trailhead: From Broadway and Mapleton Avenue in Boulder, travel west on Mapleton for 0.8 mile to the Mount Sanitas trailhead. Parking areas are on the right and left side of the road. GPS: N40 01.1464' / W105 17.4019'

The Hike

Go left and up the road, beginning a gradual climb up the Sanitas Valley. Pass the Dakota Ridge Trail on the right and continue straight on the Sanitas Valley Trail to the north. The road you are hiking on was once a wagon road used to access various quarries in the Sanitas Valley.

At around the 0.9-mile mark, the Hawthorne Trail goes right and down. Go left and up the road past a kiosk. The trail soon narrows and begins switchbacking up the east side of Mount Sanitas. Cacti, Indian paintbrushes, and other wildflowers grow profusely on this open hillside during the late spring and summer months.

The trail drops across a small gulch, then begins to climb in earnest through the rocks to the summit of Mount Sani-tas. Arrive at the summit and take a well-deserved rest. Enjoy the views east to the plains and the city of Boulder.

The loop now drops steeply down the west side of Mount Sanitas, and you lose elevation quickly. The trail is extremely rocky and can be quite icy in the winter months. At around the 2.3-mile mark, the

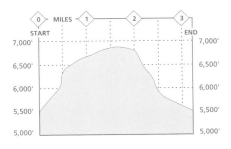

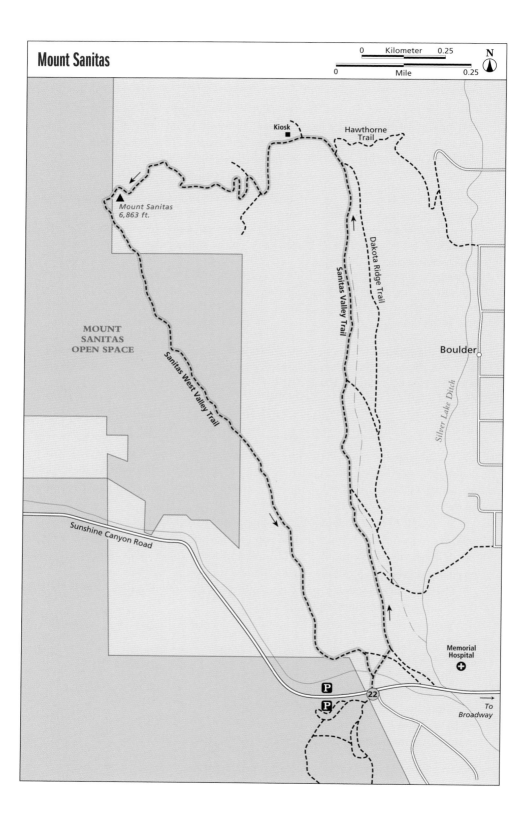

Mount Sanitas

Kiosk

Hawthorne Trail

▲ Mount Sanitas
6,863 ft.

MOUNT
SANITAS
OPEN SPACE

Sanitas Valley Trail

Dakota Ridge Trail

Sanitas West Valley Trail

Boulder

Silver Lake Ditch

Sunshine Canyon Road

Memorial
Hospital

22

To
Broadway

Kilometer

Mile

N

trail parallels short sandstone rock formations on the left. Rock climbers use these cliffs to hone their climbing skills, and the cliffs have become quite popular in recent years.

The trail continues to drop on very loose and rocky log-and-rock steps and winds around the rocks back toward the trailhead. Cross over a small wood bridge and go right to the pavilion and the end of the hike.

This is an extremely popular area with trail users and can be very crowded on weekends and late afternoons. Arrive early, or in the middle of the afternoon, to secure a parking place.

Miles and Directions

0.0 Start by walking up the wide Sanitas Valley Trail.

1.0 Arrive at a kiosk.

1.8 Arrive at the scenic summit of Mount Sanitas.

3.2 Arrive back at the parking area.

23 Bald Mountain Scenic Area

As the name suggests, this is a short, scenic hike around and up to the top of Bald Mountain (7,160 feet). There are spectacular views of the Indian Peaks and the plains. It's a great hike for the young ones.

Start: From the parking area, access the signed Pines to Peak Trail just pass the kiosk.
Distance: 1.5-mile loop
Hiking time: About 1 to 1.5 hours
Difficulty: Easy
Trail surface: Smooth
Seasons: Year-round

Other trail users: Equestrians
Canine compatibility: Dogs not permitted
Maps: Boulder County, USGS, and Boulder County Open Space/Bald Mountain map
Trail contact: City of Boulder Mountain Parks and Open Space; (303) 441-3440; www .bouldercolorado.gov

Finding the trailhead: From Broadway and Mapleton Avenue in Boulder, travel west on Mapleton, which becomes Sunshine Canyon Road, for 4.8 miles to the Bald Mountain Scenic Area trailhead and parking area on the left. GPS: N40 02.5152' / W105 20.2873'

The Hike

What a great hike to bring the kids on! It's short, there are numerous places to stop, there are picnic tables located near the trailhead, and the views are just spectacular.

From the parking area, the trail travels past an old corral and several picnic tables on a smooth, wide trail to a trail junction. The Summit Trail goes up and to the left. Go right on the Pines-to-Peak Trail and curve to the west. The trail parallels Sunshine Canyon Road for a short distance, passing through a small stand of ponderosa pines. Expect to see wildflowers during the late spring and summer months along this section of the trail.

The trail winds to the south and you are faced with breathtaking views of the southern Indian Peaks. North and South Arapaho Peaks stand tall in the southern skyline and you get a full view of Arapaho Glacier, the southernmost glacier in North America.

At around the 0.6-mile mark the trail goes back to the east through a stand of ponderosa and lodgepole pines, with a bench on the right. Continue east into an open meadow, where the trail to the summit goes up and left. There are lots of wildflowers here during the summer months.

Make a short climb, with open views in all directions, to the summit of Bald

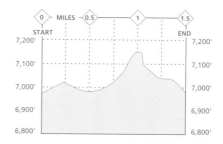

Looking west from the summit of Bald Mountain

Mountain, where a bench nestles in a cluster of ponderosa pines. Take a break and enjoy the views. The trail now drops down through the ponderosas and curves back to the east toward the trailhead. The trail passes several stately ponderosas and meets the Pines-to-Peak Trail again. Go left and back to the trailhead.

Be on the lookout for mule deer, Abert's squirrels, chipmunks, Nuttall's cottontails, magpies, and other wildlife. The corral and cattle chute near the trailhead are the remains of an old homestead from the late 1800s. Mining was done near the Bald Mountain Scenic Area, and remnants of the old Weist Brothers mines can be seen around Bald Mountain.

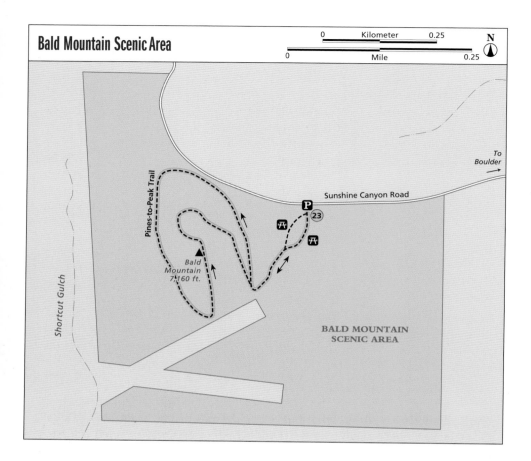

Bald Mountain Scenic Area

Miles and Directions

0.0 Start at the parking area and access the trail near the kiosk.

0.2 The trail forks; go right.

0.9 Arrive at the top of Bald Mountain and take a short rest on the bench.

1.5 Arrive back at the trailhead.

24 Betasso Preserve

The city of Boulder and the county of Boulder have done an amazing job of preserving lands in and around the city, and Betasso Preserve is one of the many open space lands that citizens of Boulder County and the Front Range can use. This hike is a nice outing through forests of ponderosa pines on a smooth well-maintained trail.

Start: From the parking area, walk east down a short hill to the signed Canyon Loop Trail.
Distance: 3.2-mile loop
Hiking time: About 1 to 1.5 hours
Difficulty: Easy
Trail surface: Smooth and well maintained by volunteers and open space rangers
Seasons: Year-round

Other trail users: Mountain bikers and equestrians
Canine compatibility: Dogs not permitted
Maps: Boulder County Open Space/Betasso Preserve map
Trail contact: Boulder County Open Space; (303) 678-6200; www.bouldercounty .org/government/dept/pages/pos.aspx

Finding the trailhead: From the junction of CO 93 (Broadway) and CO 119 (Canyon) in Boulder, go west on CO 119 toward Nederland. Go right on Sugarloaf Road and travel 0.8 mile to the turnoff for Betasso Preserve. Go right and follow signs to the trailhead, picnic area, and parking area. GPS: N40 01.2449' / W105 20.5050'

Old farming equipment

Beautiful open meadow at Betasso Preserve

The Hike

This area was first homesteaded by the Blanchard family, which worked the land for a number of years. In 1915 the family sold the ranch to Steve Betasso. The Betasso family raised cattle on the land for sixty years, and in 1975 sold the land to Boulder County to be preserved as open space. Remnants of the old homestead can be seen scattered along the trail and near the picnic area.

From the trailhead/picnic area, go left on the Canyon Loop Trail. Climb a short hill, with excellent views to the west. Reach the top of the hill and follow the trail as it drops through the trees. At around the 0.8-mile mark the trail climbs up a short hill covered with beautiful wild-flowers during the summer months. The trail goes right and switchbacks down to a small creek crossing. At around the 1.9-mile mark make a second creek crossing and begin a gentle climb through the trees.

Continue on the smooth trail and up to a gate. Numerous volunteers and open space rangers put in many

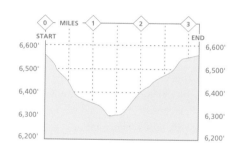

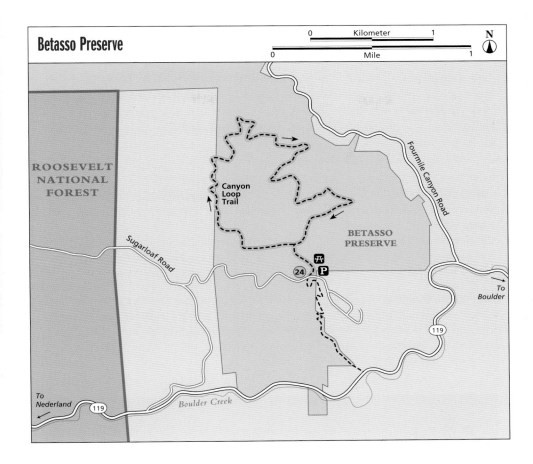

Betasso Preserve

ROOSEVELT
NATIONAL
FOREST

Canyon
Loop
Trail

Sugarloaf Road

Fourmile Canyon Road

BETASSO
PRESERVE

24

To
Boulder

119

To
Nederland

119

Boulder Creek

an hour working on the trail and bringing it to its present standard. Thanks to all
these folks for their hard work and a job well done.

At around the 2.8-mile mark, reach a gate and an old road. Follow the road back
to the trailhead and picnic area. Bring the family, pack a lunch, and enjoy this beautiful piece of open space.

Miles and Directions

0.0   Start from the parking area and access the signed Canyon Loop Trail.

0.1   Pass through a gate.

0.2   Go left following the Canyon Loop Trail.

1.6   Reach a small creek crossing.

1.9   Arrive at the second creek crossing.

2.8   Pass through a gate.

3.2   Arrive back at the trailhead.

25 Sugarloaf Mountain

This short hike up to the top of Sugarloaf Mountain (8,912 feet) offers spectacular views of the Indian Peaks Wilderness, Rocky Mountain National Park, the James Peak Wilderness Area, and the plains. Sunsets and sunrises on top of Sugarloaf Mountain are not to be missed. Doing the hike at these times will reward you with a beautiful show of nature's light.

Start: From the parking area, access the trail just past two metal posts.
Distance: 2.2 miles out and back
Hiking time: About 1 to 2 hours
Difficulty: Moderate
Trail surface: Follows an old, rocky mining road
Seasons: Year-round

Other trail users: None
Canine compatibility: Dogs not permitted
Maps: Trails Illustrated Indian Peaks/Gold Hill #104
Trail contact: Boulder County Parks; (303) 678-6200; www.bouldercounty.org/government/dept/pages/pos.aspx

Finding the trailhead: From the junction of CO 93 (Broadway) and CO 119 (Canyon) in Boulder, go west on CO 119 for 5.5 miles to Sugarloaf Road. Turn right on Sugarloaf Road and travel 4.5 miles to a turnoff on the right for the Switzerland Trailhead. Go right for 1 mile up to the trailhead and a parking area. The hike starts here. GPS: N40 01.2965' / W105 25.2929'

Moon setting from the summit of Sugarloaf Mountain

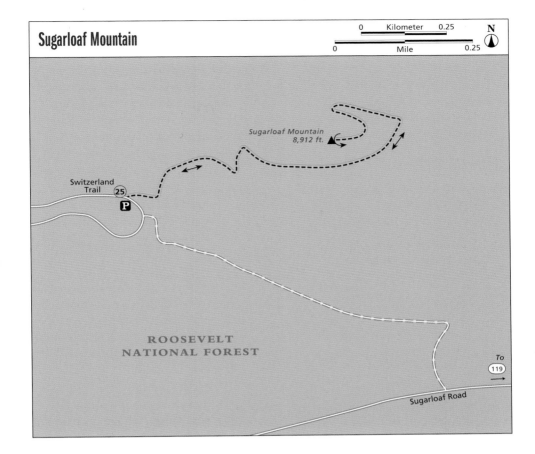

Sugarloaf Mountain

Switzerland Trail (25)

Sugarloaf Mountain
8,912 ft.

ROOSEVELT
NATIONAL FOREST

Sugarloaf Road

To
(119)

The Hike

From the parking area look to the east for an old road with two metal posts and a cable going across it. Travel past the cable and begin climbing on the rough old road. Ponderosa pines, Douglas firs, and small aspen trees line the trail through this section. From Boulder, the top of Sugarloaf Mountain looks stark and barren, but that's not the case on the western side of the mountain, which is covered by various trees and wildflowers.

Continue up to the first of several switchbacks that force the trail to the east and south. At around the 0.8-mile mark, pass a sign on the left. At this point you'll see the first indications of the Sugarloaf fire, which charred many acres on the east and south sides of the mountain. Burned and twisted pines are scattered along the steep slope of the mountain and lend an eerie feel to this section of the trail.

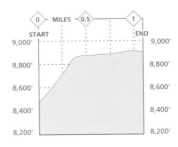

The trail cuts straight across a scree slope and makes a sharp left up to the summit. Spectacular views of the Indian Peaks and Rocky Mountain National Park smack you right in the face at the sharp turn and make a good reason to stop and enjoy. Heading back west, the trail soon gains the summit and you are rewarded with spectacular views in all directions. If you time your hike right and arrive around sunset, you will enjoy a beautiful show and breathtaking light.

Enjoy the views before heading back down the trail to the parking area.

Miles and Directions

0.0 Start by passing the gate and heading up the old rough road.

0.6 Arrive at series of steep switchbacks.

0.8 Arrive at a Sugarloaf Mountain sign on the left.

1.1 Top of Sugarloaf Mountain.

2.2 Arrive back at the trailhead.

26 Davidson Mesa Open Space

This great hike is within the city limits of Louisville. It offers great views to the Flatirons, the Indian Peaks, and Longs Peak to the north. Bring the dog; there is an enclosed dog run where your pooch can play.

Start: From the parking area, walk west on the wide trail just past the kiosk.
Distance: 3.3-mile loop
Hiking time: About 1 to 1.5 hours
Difficulty: Easy to moderate
Trail surface: Mostly flat and hardpacked
Seasons: Year-round; can be snow-packed in the winter months

Other trail users: Mountain bikers and equestrians
Canine compatibility: Dogs must be on leash outside of the dog run area
Maps: City of Louisville Open Space map
Trail contact: City of Louisville; (303) 335-4729

Finding the trailhead: From the intersection of McCaslin Boulevard and US 36, go north on McCaslin Boulevard for 1.5 miles to the trailhead on the left, at the top of hill. GPS: N39 58.4150' / W105 09.5885'

The Hike

This is a great little hike with fantastic views to the west and north. It's mostly flat, leading through beautiful open grasslands with lots of birds, coyotes, and hawks.

Follow the obvious trail from the kiosk and enjoy spectacular views to the west. Arrive at a trail junction near US 36. Go right, and then follow the nice trail to a junction near some houses. Go right and hug the fence line, and then veer left, drop down a steep hill, and reach the Davidson ditch. Go right along the ditch and then up a steep hill to a junction near the dog run. Continue straight and arrive back at the parking area.

This is a popular area with dog owners. All dogs must be on leash when outside of the dog run. Please pick up all droppings.

Miles and Directions

0.0 Start from parking area, read the informative kiosk, and then head west toward the Flatirons.
1.5 Reach a trail junction and US 36. Go right.
2.2 Go right as the trail hugs a fence line with houses on the left.
2.6 Go left, and then drop down a short hill.
2.8 Go right along the Davidson ditch.
3.1 Reach a junction and dog run. Go straight back to the parking area.
3.3 Arrive back at the trailhead and parking area.

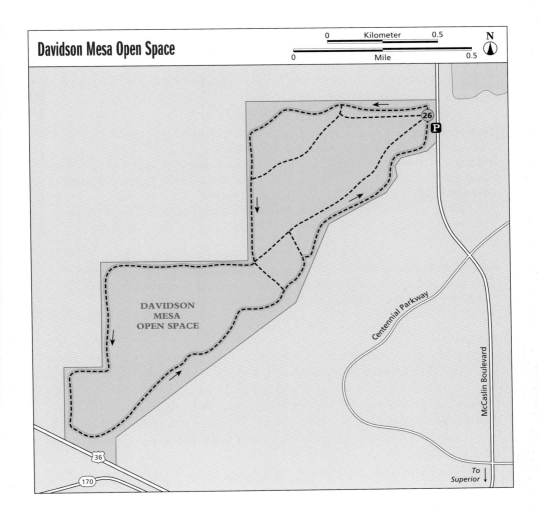

Davidson Mesa Open Space

DAVIDSON
MESA
OPEN SPACE

Centennial Parkway

McCaslin Boulevard

To
Superior

Spectacular views from the trailhead

27 Coalton Trail

This trailhead, established in 2011, offers several options for hiking on the high prairie near the town of Superior.

Start: From the parking area, walk west on the obvious wide trail past a gate.
Distance: 5.8 miles out and back
Hiking time: About 2 to 3 hours
Difficulty: Moderate
Trail surface: Hardpacked and mostly smooth
Seasons: Year-round; can be snow-packed in the winter months

Other trail users: Mountain bikers and equestrian
Canine compatibility: Dogs must be on leash
Maps: Boulder County Open Space Coalton Trailhead map
Trail contact: Boulder County Open Space; (303) 499-3675; http://townofsuperior .com/

Finding the trailhead: From the intersection of McCaslin Boulevard and US 36 go south on McCaslin Boulevard for 1.5 miles to the trailhead on the right at the bottom of the hill and turn right into the trailhead parking area. GPS: N39 55.4423' / W105 09.5887'

The Hike

This new trailhead has several different options for an enjoyable day of hiking in the high open prairie near the town of Superior. The hike described here takes the Coalton Trail up to a junction with the High Prairie Trail, where you can easily turn this outing into a beautiful 10.8 mile out-and-back hike. Park in the trailhead parking lot (new in 2011), with bathrooms and picnic tables, and access the Coalton Trail at the fence line.

Pass the Meadowlark Trail on the right, staying on the Coalton Trail, and enjoy easy hiking for a mile or so to a short, steep hill. Climb the hill for a short distance to a flat area.

At the 1.6-mile mark, the trail makes a sharp left and heads in a southerly direction, with a fence line on both sides. Enjoy spectacular open views to the Flatirons to the west; be on the lookout for coyotes, birds of prey, and the ever-present meadowlarks.

At the 2.3-mile mark the trail goes right, heading directly west with views of the open prairie, the Flatirons, the Continental Divide, and the massive wind turbines of the National Wind Technology Center.

Reach the trail junction with High Prairie Trail and the turnaround point at 2.9 miles. Retrace your steps to the trailhead.

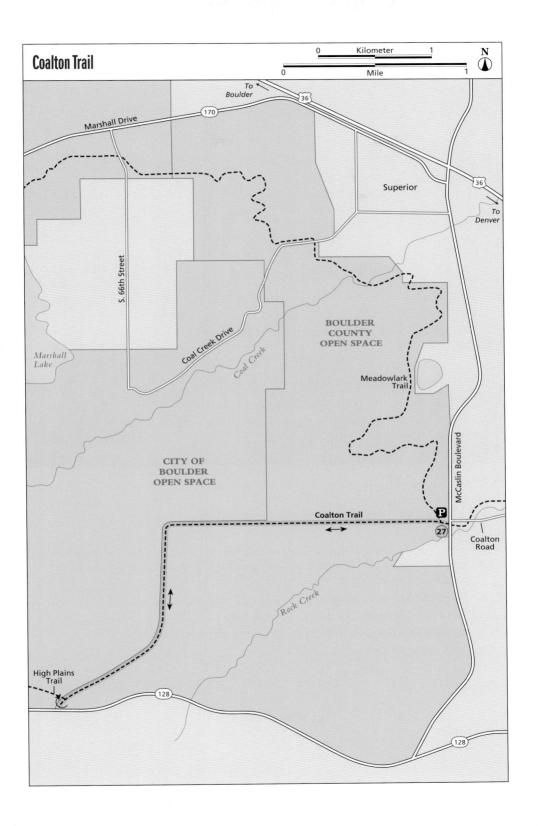

A runner on the new trail

Miles and Directions

0.0   From the trailhead, take the obvious trail leading west into open prairie, passing the new Meadowlark Trail on the right.

1.6   The trail goes left at the powerlines.

2.3   The trail veers right with open views to the south and west.

2.9   Arrive at a junction with the High Prairie Trail and the turnaround point.

5.8   Arrive back at the trailhead.

28 Gregory Canyon/Green Mountain Loop

Another gem in Boulder Mountain Parks system, this loop offers a great outing up a beautiful canyon, with views to the east, west, and north.

Start: From the parking area, walk west to the signed Gregory Canyon Trail.
Distance: 3.1-mile loop
Hiking time: About 1.5 to 2.0 hours
Difficulty: Moderate to strenuous
Trail surface: Rocky and steep for most of the loop

Seasons: Year-round
Other trail users: None
Canine compatibility: Dogs must be on leash
Maps: USGS Eldorado Springs CO
Trail contact: City of Boulder Mountain Parks and Open Space; (303) 441-3440; www .bouldercolorado.gov

Finding the trailhead: From the junction of Broadway and Baseline Road in Boulder, go west on Baseline (toward Flagstaff Mountain) for 1.4 miles to the Gregory Canyon trailhead and parking area. GPS: N39 59.5115' / W105 17.3398'

The Hike

From the parking area/trailhead, follow the sign for the Gregory Canyon Trail, heading west through thick vegetation. Within a short distance you will arrive at a junction with the Saddle Rock Trail on the left. This is the return of the loop. Bear right, following the Gregory Canyon Trail and climbing at a modest grade. Good views of sandstone rocks appear, with lush vegetation down and to the left along the drainage.

The trail becomes rocky the higher you climb, with great views back to Boulder and the east. After 1 mile and 900 feet of elevation gain, the trail reaches a ridge and skirts through a beautiful forest of ponderosa pine and Douglas fir. Make a small drop to a stream on the left and an old road on the right. This lovely, small, open meadow has beautiful, large ferns and alpine flowers blooming along the trail in the summer months.

Go left up to the Green Mountain Lodge, a restroom, a picnic table, a kiosk, and a trail junction. From the lodge, follow the E. M. Greenman Trail up into a forest of ponderosa and lodgepole pines. The trail becomes quite narrow and rocky, climbing steeply to a junction with the Saddle Rock Trail at 1.7 miles.

Go left onto the Saddle Rock Trail (going right will take you to the top of Green Mountain, 8,144 feet, in another 1.3

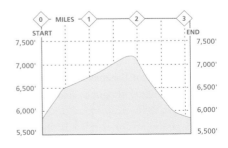

Janet and Laurel out for an early fall hike

miles). Follow the rocky tread, with views back west to the Indian Peaks, and north to Mount Meeker (13,911 feet) and Longs Peak (14,255 feet).

At the 1.9-mile mark the trail drops quite dramatically into Gregory Canyon. Certain portions of the trail are very steep, so use caution when descending. There are great views again to the east, with a spectacular view of the University of Colorado campus and the plains.

At the 2.7-mile mark the trail makes a sharp right along a small drainage and drops steeply back to the parking area, completing the loop.

This is a very popular trail and sees a lot of use by hikers, trail runners, and bird watchers. Dogs are allowed but must be kept on a leash or under strict voice command. Do not cut switchbacks or make new trails, and yield to the uphill hiker.

Miles and Directions

0.0   Start at the parking area and access the well-marked Gregory Canyon Trail.

1.2   Arrive at a junction with Green Mountain Lodge and E. M. Greenman Trail.

1.7   Arrive at a junction with Saddle Rock Trail.

3.1   Arrive back at the trailhead.

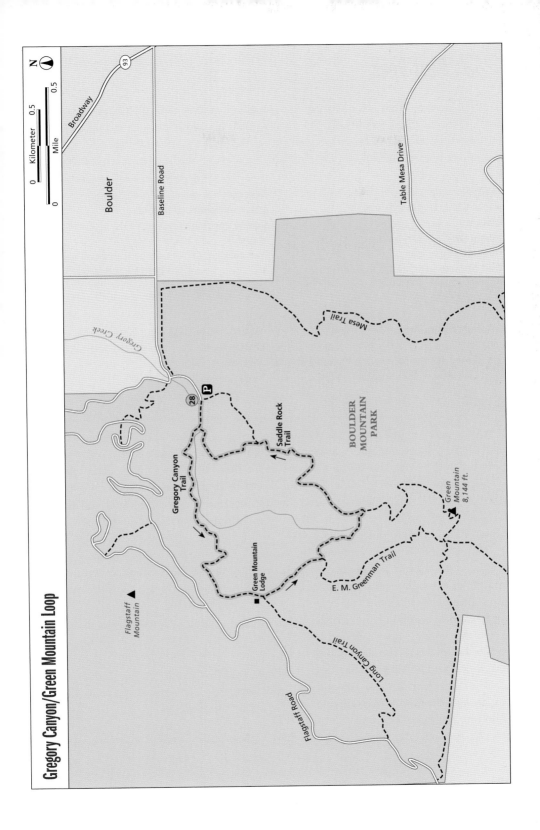

Gregory Canyon/Green Mountain Loop

29 Bear Peak

This is a strenuous but great hike up to the summit of Bear Peak (8,461 feet), one of Boulder's most visible landmarks. The Bear Peak Trail follows Bear Creek up beautiful Bear Canyon, then makes a steep ascent up the Bear Peak West Ridge Trail to the summit. Expect beautiful vistas and blooming wildflowers during the summer months.

Start: From the parking area, walk west to the signed Walter Orr-Roberts Trail.
Distance: 7.4-mile loop
Hiking time: About 4 to 5 hours
Difficulty: Strenuous
Trail surface: Well-traveled and smooth up to the Bear Canyon Trail. From there on the trail is rocky and steep.

Seasons: Year-round
Other trail users: Equestrians
Canine compatibility: Dogs must be on leash
Maps: USGS Eldorado Springs CO
Trail contact: City of Boulder Mountain Parks and Open Space; (303) 441-3440; www .bouldercolorado.gov

Finding the trailhead: From the junction of Broadway and Table Mesa Road in Boulder, go west on Table Mesa for 2.4 miles to the National Center for Atmospheric Research (NCAR), where you'll find parking and the trailhead. GPS: N39 58.4465' / W105 16.2840'

The Hike

From the parking area, access the Walter Orr-Roberts Weather Trail on the west side of NCAR. Follow this informative trail for a short 0.2 mile to a kiosk and a sign pointing to the Mesa Trail. Drop a short distance, then climb steeply to a water tower.

From the water tower follow signs for the Mesa Trail, staying left at all trail junctions. At the 1.2-mile mark you arrive at the junction of the Mesa Trail and Bear Creek. Go left up the steep, wide road to a junction with Mesa Trail and the Bear Canyon Trail on the right.

Go right on the Bear Canyon Trail, passing a utility tower and power lines. The trail becomes rockier and begins to climb steeply. It crosses Bear Creek several times and winds through several patches of aspens, willows, and cottonwoods. Wildflowers grow profusely along the creek, as do ferns and other flowering shrubs.

At the 3.1-mile mark you arrive at a beautiful, small meadow and a trail junction. The Green–Bear Trail goes to the right. You go left and up on the Bear Peak West Ridge Trail into the pines. The trail climbs steeply through the pines to an

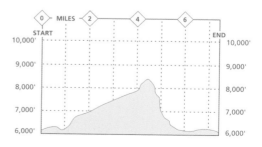

Awesome views from the summit of Bear Peak

open area at an old fence line. The trail cuts to the left and away from private property. Here views open to the west to Walker Ranch Open Space, the Indian Peaks, and Mount Meeker (13,911 feet) to the north.

The trail begins to climb a steep hillside with numerous granite boulders. At around the 4.2-mile mark the trail forks to the left, climbing a series of steep, granite steps. Before you know it you are standing below the pointed summit of Bear Peak. Follow the trail through the rocks to the north ridge, past the Fern Canyon Trail, and scramble up the north ridge to the summit proper. Take a long rest and enjoy the spectacular views in all directions.

After your rest and photo session, go back down the ridge to the Fern Canyon Trail. Go right and down the very steep Fern Canyon Trail to a saddle. The trail is loose and rocky and drops over 2,000 feet in 1.4 miles, a real knee tweaker. Fern Canyon is a narrow, densely vegetated canyon filled with spectacular rock formations, aspens, and pine trees. The trail in several sections is made of steep steps and wood stairs.

The trail breaks out of the narrow canyon and you arrive at a junction with Shanahan North Trail. Continue straight on the Fern Canyon Trail, dropping to the Mesa Trail. Wildflowers bloom along the trail and in the open areas. Go left on the Mesa Trail, down to Bear Creek. From here, retrace your route back to NCAR and the parking area.

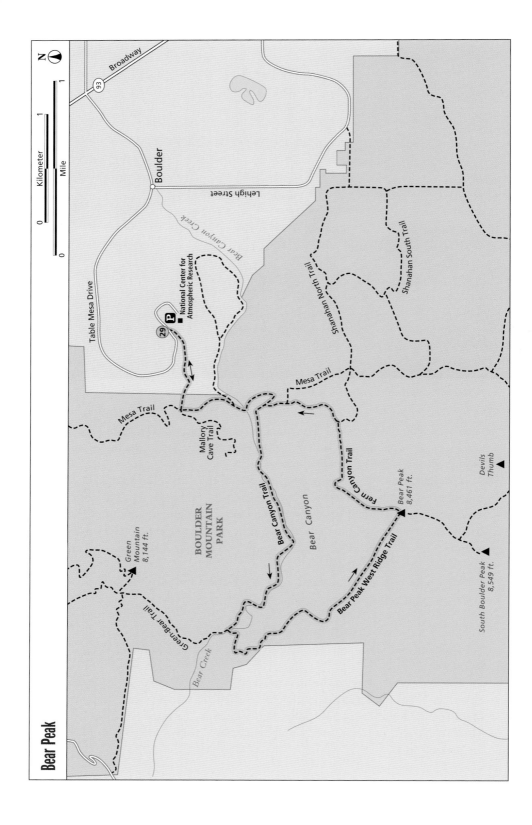

Bear Peak

N

Miles and Directions

0.0 Start behind NCAR on the Walter Orr-Roberts Trail.

0.2 Arrive at a kiosk and sign for the Mesa Trail.

0.7 Pass a very large water tank.

1.2 Arrive at a Junction with the Mesa Trail and Bear Creek.

1.4 Arrive at a junction with Bear Canyon Trail.

3.1 Arrive at a junction with Green-Bear Trail.

4.7 Arrive at the spectacular summit of Bear Peak.

4.8 Arrive at a junction with Fern Canyon Trail.

5.6 Arrive at a junction with Shanahan North Trail.

6.0 arrive back at a junction with Mesa Trail.

7.4 Arrive back at NCAR, the trailhead, and the parking area.

30 Meyers Homestead Trail

This peaceful hike follows an old fire road past an old homestead, and through open meadows and stands of ponderosas, Douglas firs, and quaking aspens.

Start: From the parking area, walk north to signed Meyers Homestead Trail.
Distance: 5.2 miles out and back
Hiking time: About 2.5 to 3.5 hours
Difficulty: Moderate
Trail surface: Smooth
Seasons: Year-round

Other trail users: Mountain bikers and equestrians
Canine compatibility: Dogs must be on leash
Maps: Boulder County Open Space/Walker Ranch map
Trail contact: Boulder County Open Space; 303-678-6200; www.bouldercounty .org/government/dept/pages/pos.aspx

Finding the trailhead: From the intersection of Broadway and Baseline Road in Boulder, travel west on Baseline, which becomes Flagstaff Road, for 7.5 miles to the Meyers Open Space parking area on the right. The hike starts here. GPS: N39 57.3271' / W105 20.1664'

The Hike

From the parking area, access the wide Meyers Homestead Trail near the kiosk. Follow the trail down into an open meadow. Remnants of a recent fire can be seen on the hillside to the left. The trail drops into a narrow meadow, with the old Meyers Homestead on the left. The homestead is all that is left of a thriving cattle ranch that dates back to the late 1800s.

Past the homestead the trail climbs a short hill, with a small stream on the left. Thick willows line the banks of the stream, along with aspens and other water-loving plants. The hillside on the right of the trail is covered with granite boulders, widely spaced ponderosas, and blooming wildflowers (during the summer months).

The trail passes an old fire road at the 1.3-mile mark and then climbs a short steep hill. Pleasant hiking leads you up past a steep, forested hillside on the left and open area on the right to a beautiful young aspen forest at the 1.8-mile mark. The trail climbs steeply through the aspens and reaches a beautiful open meadow at the

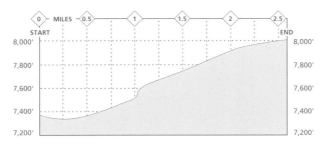

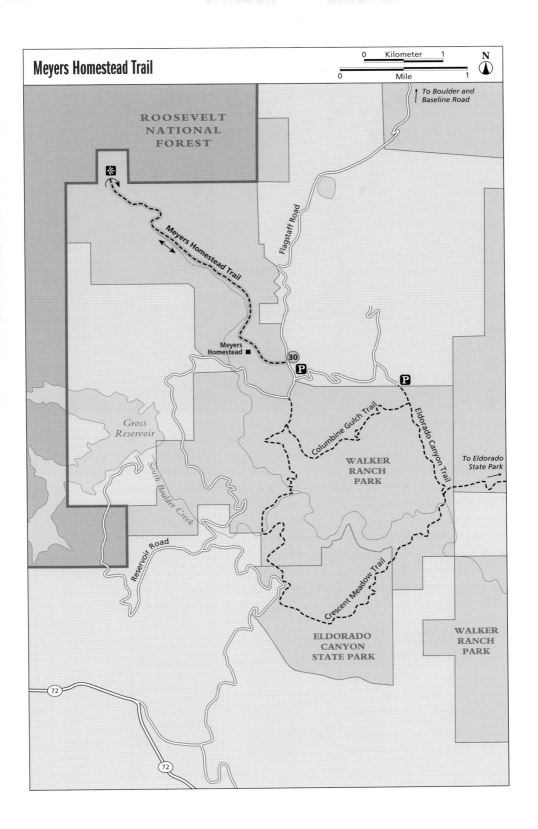

Blooming Globeflower

2.1-mile mark. The meadow is filled with tall grasses; there is a small stream lined with willows and aspen trees on the left. The meadow is also filled with various wildflowers during the summer months and is a great spot to take a break and enjoy the serene setting.

The trail climbs at a gentle grade through the meadow, then reaches a flat area at the crest of the hill. Great views open to the north and east to Boulder. The trail heads sharply to the left, and soon reaches the overlook and the turnaround point of the hike. Enjoy the views of Sugarloaf Mountain (8,912 feet) and Boulder Canyon.

After a short break, turn around and retrace your route to the trailhead.

Miles and Directions

0.0 Start by passing the kiosk and heading down the Meyers Homestead Trail.

0.5 Reach the old Meyers Homestead.

1.3 Arrive at an old service road junction.

1.8 Arrive at a beautiful aspen forest.

2.6 Arrive at the overlook and turnaround point.

5.2 Arrive back at the trailhead.

31 Walker Ranch

This popular hike leads around the old homestead of James Walker. Beautiful views, excellent wildflowers, and good fishing along South Boulder Creek are the main attractions on this hike. Fly fishing is excellent along several sections of South Boulder Creek.

Start: From the parking area, walk past the kiosk and through a gate to the start of the trail.
Distance: 7.4-mile loop
Hiking time: About 3 to 4.5 hours
Difficulty: Moderate
Trail surface: Extremely rocky in places
Seasons: Year-round

Other trail users: Mountain bikers and equestrians
Canine compatibility: Dogs must be on leash
Maps: USGS Boulder County; Boulder County Open Space/Walker Ranch map
Trail contact: Boulder County Open Space; (303) 678-6200; www.bouldercounty.org/ government/dept/pages/pos.aspx

Finding the trailhead: From the intersection of Broadway and Baseline Road in Boulder, travel 7.5 miles west on Baseline, which becomes Flagstaff Road and climbs up past Flagstaff Mountain. Turn left into the South Boulder Creek trailhead and parking area at Walker Ranch. GPS: N39 57.0456' / W105 20.1468'

The Hike

From the trailhead, go through the gate and begin a nice descent to South Boulder Creek. The Walker Ranch Loop Trail follows an old road and passes several rock formations on the right. At the bottom of the hill, cross a small stream and then go right along beautiful South Boulder Creek.

The trail goes upstream to a bridge. Cross the bridge and go left up the steep hill. Crest the steep part of the hill, where the trail bends to the right, and enjoy excellent views to the west. This trail is extremely popular with mountain bikers, so be aware of their presence, especially on weekends.

The trail becomes level just past a small rock garden and travels past a gate and down through a beautiful forested area. Climb up a hill and through another gate, where the trail drops you onto Reservoir Road. Go left up the road for 0.1 mile to a trail on the left. Go left up the trail and arrive at Crescent Meadows. Go left on the Walker Ranch Loop Trail heading to the east and

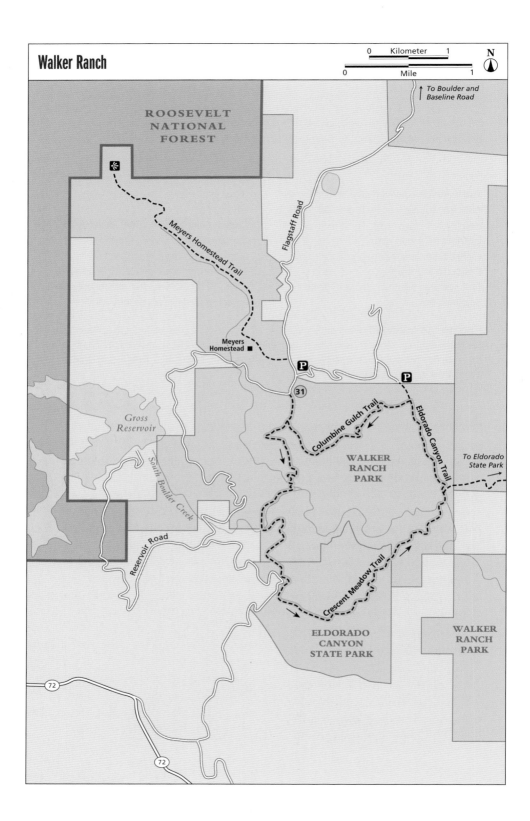

through the open meadow. There are great views to the west, and wildflowers light up the meadow in late spring and early summer.

At around the 3.5-mile mark, the trail leads you into a dense forest and starts to drop in elevation. Travel past several rocky sections and through a small, open meadow. Arrive at a sign warning mountain bikers to dismount. Follow rock-and-log steps steeply down to South Boulder Creek and a bridge. This is a good spot to take a break and admire the scenery. South Boulder Creek runs wild through this section, and the deep pools of water are crystal clear and are excellent for fly fishing.

A young deer getting its new antlers

Cross the bridge and go left, passing the Eldorado Canyon Trail on the right. Begin a good climb through the ponderosa and spruce trees to a junction with the Columbine Gulch Trail at the 5.8-mile mark. Go left on this narrow trail into a narrow, forested gulch. Pass a small stream, then begin a steep ascent past several switchbacks. A beautiful stretch brings you up and out of the gulch to a ridge and excellent views. Go right and up a gentle grade, following the Columbine Gulch Trail past a recent burn area and back to the trailhead.

Once the site of the largest cattle ranch on the Front Range, Walker Ranch is now a beautiful piece of open space land that provides a glimpse into Boulder County history. James Walker first came to the area for health reasons, and thrived in the fresh mountain air and peaceful setting of open meadows and mountain terrain. Hope you do the same on this hike.

Miles and Directions

- **0.0** Start from the parking area and pass through a gate at the kiosk.
- **1.0** Cross over a small stream crossing.
- **1.5** Bridge over South Boulder Creek.
- **2.4** Pass Reservoir Road.
- **4.5** Begin a serious steep, rocky descent.
- **4.7** Cross a bridge over South Boulder Creek.
- **5.8** Go left on the Columbine Gulch Trail.
- **7.4** Arrive back at the trailhead.

32 Walden Ponds Wildlife Area

A wonderful family hike circles around several ponds, with spectacular views of the Indian Peaks. The boardwalk along Cottonwood Marsh has several interpretive signs and is a great place to bring the kids for an educational hike. Walden Ponds is also a stopover for migratory birds and offers a great opportunity to view waterfowl, songbirds, and various mammals.

Start: From the parking area, walk west to the signed Boardwalk trail.
Distance: 2.1-mile loop
Hiking time: About 1 to 2 hours
Difficulty: Easy
Trail surface: Smooth, well maintained
Seasons: Year-round

Other trail users: Mountain bikers
Canine compatibility: Dogs not permitted
Maps: Boulder County Open Space/Walden Ponds map
Trail contact: Boulder County Open Space; (303) 678-6200; www.bouldercounty .org/government/dept/pages/pos.aspx

Finding the trailhead: From the intersection of US 36 (28th Street) and CO 7 (Arapahoe Avenue) in Boulder, travel east on CO 7 for 5 miles to 75th Street. Go left on 75th Street for 2 miles to the entrance of the Walden Ponds open space area. Turn left and travel 0.2 mile to the Cottonwood Marsh picnic area and trailhead. GPS: N40 02.3949' / W105 11.1813'

The Hike

The hike starts at the Cottonwood Marsh picnic area and quickly accesses the boardwalk, which has several interpretive signs explaining the geology and history of the area. The boardwalk cuts through a marshy area with tall cattails and thick marsh grasses.

After the boardwalk the trail meets a service road and travels up toward the ranger field station. Go left, up through a fence line to a kiosk and the first of the Sawhill Ponds. Go right at the kiosk and begin the start of the loop around Sawhill Ponds. Be on the lookout for waterfowl and high-flying raptors. Fishing is permitted in the ponds, and several side trails access the ponds.

The trail goes west, with amazing views of the majestic Indian Peaks. Pelican Marsh, Island Lake, and Bass Pond are on your right. Trails access this area, so if you have the time feel free to explore. At around the 0.9-mile mark the trail goes to the left and into a stand of tall cottonwoods and thick Russian olive trees.

Walden Ponds is in a constant state of flux, and a huge effort

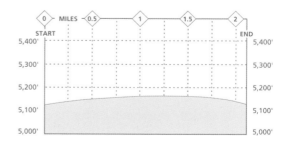

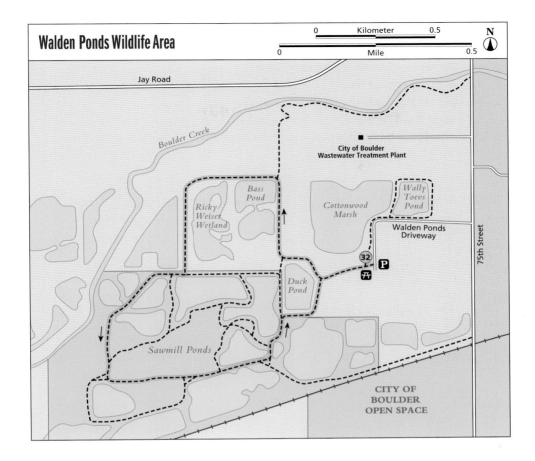

has been put forth to restore the area to its natural state. Once the site of a gravel operation for the county of Boulder, as little as thirty years ago the land at Walden Ponds was open pits and stagnant, still water. In 1974 Boulder County, with support from citizens, started an aggressive program of reclamation. Pit runs were shaped and formed into ponds and small islands. Water was diverted to establish ponds, and tree and shrub seedlings were planted to enhance natural vegetation. What you see today is an ongoing effort to create a viable and aesthetically pleasing plant and wildlife habitat. Tall marsh grasses, cattails, and muskrat dens are off to the left. A large, sun-bleached cottonwood on the right is a favorite perch for birds of prey. Keep an eye open for these beautiful birds, which hunt the small rodents and cottontail rabbits that call Walden Ponds home.

At around the 1.5-mile mark the trail curves back to the east, toward a viewing blind. Go left at the blind and follow the trail along a fence line, with Duck Pond on your right.

Back at the kiosk retrace your route back to the picnic area and the parking lot.

Miles and Directions

0.0 Start on the boardwalk at Cottonwood Marsh.

0.2 Arrive at the Sawhill Ponds.

0.9 Bear left at the fence line.

1.7 Go left at viewing blind.

2.1 Arrive back at the trailhead.

33 Marshall Mesa

A beautiful Front Range hike with a great trail system and wonderful vistas in a park-like setting.

Start: From the parking area, walk south through a gate to the start of the trail.
Distance: 3.3-mile loop
Hiking time: About 1.5 to 3 hours
Difficulty: Moderate
Trail surface: Smooth and hard packed with short rocky sections
Seasons: Year-round; can be snow packed in winter months

Other trail users: Mountain bikers and equestrians
Canine compatibility: Dogs must be on leash or voice control
Maps: Boulder County Open Space/Marshall Mesa
Trail contact: Boulder County Open Space; (303) 678-6200; www.bouldercounty.org/government/dept/pages/pos.aspx

Finding the trailhead: From Boulder access Broadway (CO 93) south to the intersection with Marshall Road (CO 170). Go left on Marshall Road and make a quick right into the trailhead/parking area. GPS: N40 39.6486' / W105 51.3089'

The Hike

Start from the trailhead parking area and south into an open field on the Marshall Valley Trail. Hike through cactus, prairie grass and yucca to a trail junction at a wooden bridge. Follow the Community Ditch Trail up a short hill with great views to the east, west and north. Arrive at the top of the hill and panoramic views. Go right following the Community Ditch Trail enjoying great views and following the ditch on the left. This is a great place to let the dog swim on hot summer days. Pass several trail junctions staying on the Community Ditch Trail to a junction with the Coal Seam Trail. Go right on this beautiful trail enjoying wildflowers during the spring and summer months. Arrive back at the trailhead and parking area.

This is a very popular hiking and biking trail in the Boulder area. It can be extremely busy during the weekends. Get to the parking early and be respectful of other trail users. Share the trail and be courteous; a smile to fellow users goes a long way.

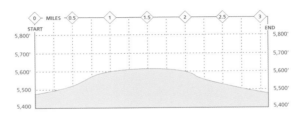

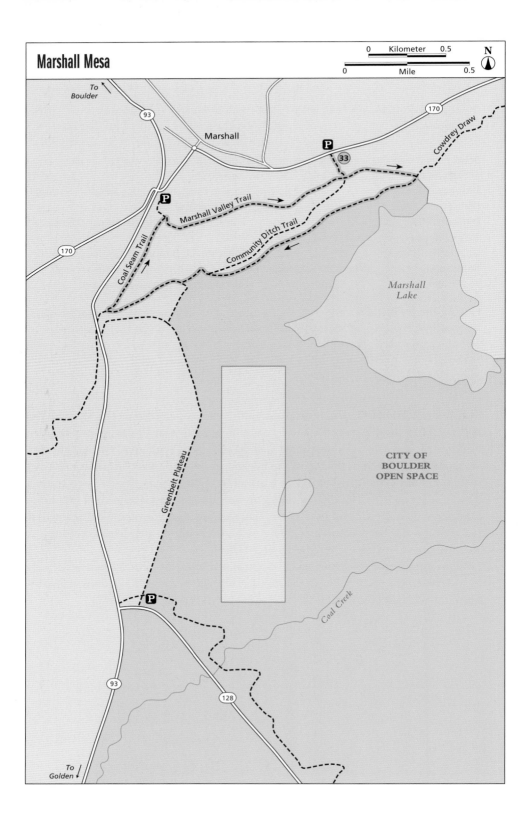

Marshall Mesa

0 Kilometer 0.5

0 Mile 0.5

N

To Boulder

93

Marshall

170

P

33

Cowdrey Draw

P

Marshall Valley Trail

Coal Seam Trail

Community Ditch Trail

Marshall Lake

170

Greenbelt Plateau

CITY OF BOULDER OPEN SPACE

Coal Creek

P

93

128

To Golden

Out for a summer hike on this awesome trail system

Miles and Directions

0.0 From the parking area head south and access the Marshall Valley Trail. Follow the Marshall Valley Trail left into an open field.

0.9 Reach a junction with the Community Ditch Trail just past a bridge. Veer right on the Community Ditch Trail and climb a hill to a trail junction.

1.2 Arrive at a trail junction; go right following the Community Ditch Trail.

1.4 Continue straight on the Community Ditch Trail.

2.2 Continue straight on the Community Ditch Trail.

2.3 Arrive at a junction with the Greenbelt Trail. Continue straight on the Community Ditch Trail.

2.7 Arrive at a junction with the Coal Seam Trail. Go right on the Coal Seam Trail.

3.3 Arrive back at the trailhead/parking area.

34 Doudy Draw Trail

A beautiful hike heads up a wide draw filled with tall prairie grasses, western wheatgrass, yuccas, wildflowers, ponderosa pines, and cottonwood trees, with spectacular views of the Flatirons.

Start: From the parking area, walk south past the kiosk and through a gate to the start of the trail.
Distance: 6.8 miles out and back
Hiking time: About 3 to 4 hours
Difficulty: Easy to moderate
Trail surface: Mostly smooth and free of rocks
Seasons: Year-round; can be extremely muddy after any precipitation

Other trail users: Mountain bikers and equestrians
Canine compatibility: Dogs not permitted
Maps: USGS Boulder County; City of Boulder Open Space/Doudy Draw map
Trail contact: City of Boulder Open Space; (303) 441-3440; www.boulder colorado.gov

Finding the trailhead: From the intersection of Broadway and Baseline in Boulder, travel south on Broadway (CO 93) to CO 170. Go right on CO 170 for 1.5 miles to the Doudy Draw Trailhead and parking area on the left. GPS: N39 56.1737' / W105 15.2380'

The Hike

From the parking area, pass through a gate and travel up the paved, handicapped-accessible Doudy Draw Trail to the Doudy Draw picnic area. Travel past the picnic area on the left, and the restrooms on the right, over a small creek lined with thick cottonwood trees. These water-loving trees are quite beautiful, and in the fall add dramatic golden color to the already colorful landscape.

At around the 0.5-mile mark the Community Ditch Trail comes in from the right, just before a bridge. The Community Ditch Trail goes to the east, along the ditch, up to CO 93. Continue straight on Doudy Draw Trail over the bridge and through the first gate. Please close the gate behind you. Drop to a seasonal stream crossing. Willows, wildflowers, and tall prairie grasses grow along the creek and are quite beautiful during the late spring and early summer months.

The trail travels up an open area past two gates, with dramatic views to the west and of the Flatirons. Looking directly west to Eldorado Canyon, you can catch a quick glimpse of the tall peaks along the Continental Divide. Past the third gate, the trail cuts across the creek

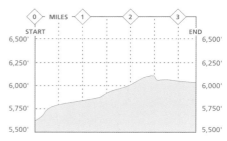

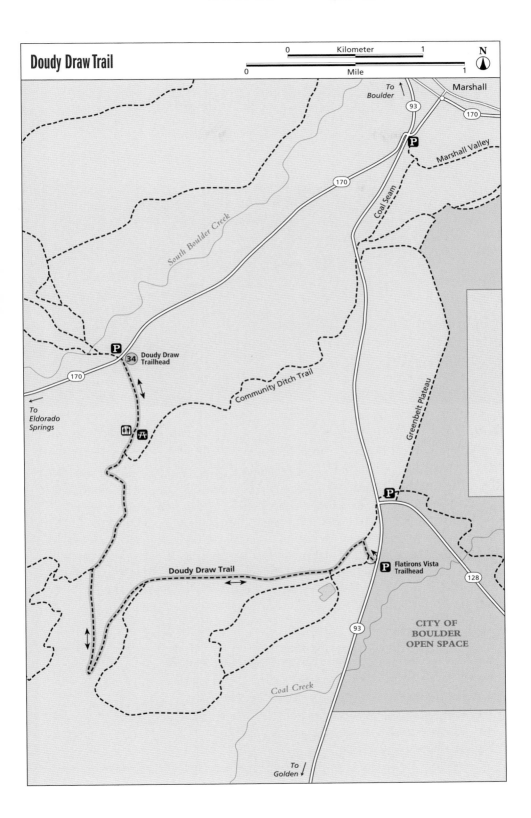

Looking east along the trail

and starts to climb into the ponderosas, and toward a ridge. Follow a long switchback to the ridge and enjoy shaded hiking through the ponderosa. The trail becomes a little rocky; looking back, the views become more open to the west and north.

This section of the trail marks the border of prairie grassland and the forest. The hiking is level and enjoyable as you pass under power lines. Reach an open area around the 2.6-mile mark, where the trail turns into an old service road. Follow the road, with views to the east, south, and north. The trail soon drops to the Flatirons Vista Trailhead, and the turnaround point of this hike. Retrace your route to the Doudy Draw Trailhead, and enjoy downhill hiking with fantastic views to the west and north.

Miles and Directions

0.0 Start from the large parking area passing through a gate at the kiosk.

0.4 Arrive at a very pleasant picnic area.

0.5 Arrive at a trail junction with the Community Ditch Trail.

1.6 Arrive at start of the somewhat long hill.

3.4 Flatirons Vista Trailhead. Retrace your steps.

6.8 Arrive back at the trailhead.

35 Rattlesnake Gulch

This is a short, steep hike up a beautiful narrow gulch, with views of towering rock walls and the Indian Peaks, in beautiful Eldorado Canyon State Park.

Start: From the parking area, walk west up the wide dirt road. Be careful of car traffic.
Distance: 5.3-mile loop
Hiking time: About 2 to 3 hours
Difficulty: Easy to moderate
Trail surface: Start of hike follows a dirt road; becomes rocky as you climb up Rattlesnake Gulch.

Seasons: Year-round; can be snowy and icy on the north-facing slopes in winter
Other trail users: Mountain bikers and equestrian
Canine compatibility: Dogs must be on leash
Maps: USGS Boulder County; Colorado State Parks/Eldorado Canyon State Park map
Trail contact: Colorado State Parks; (303) 866-3437; www.parks.state.co.us

Finding the trailhead: From the intersection of Broadway and Baseline in Boulder, travel south on Broadway (CO 93) to CO 170. Go right on CO 170 for 4.4 miles to the entrance station and parking area for Eldorado Canyon State Park. GPS: N39 55.4619' / W105 17.2472'

The Hike

Eldorado Canyon State Park is located 7 miles from downtown Boulder, and offers great outdoor recreation and spectacular scenery close to an ever-encroaching urban area. This is one of two hikes in Eldorado Canyon State Park that are great little getaways, offering year-round hiking in a beautiful state park.

From the parking area/fee station, head west up the dirt road. Pass a towering rock wall on the left: the Bastille. Take time to look at the rock climbers, then continue straight up the road, with South Boulder Creek on your right. Gold and brown rock walls are on the right and offer some of the best rock climbing in America.

At the 0.6-mile mark go left on the Fowler Trail. After a short distance go right on the Rattlesnake Gulch Trail, and climb at a gentle grade on a narrow rocky trail into a V-shaped gulch filled with aspens, willows, and wildflowers. Cross over a seasonal creek and begin a steep climb up the east side of the gulch on a rocky, narrow trail.

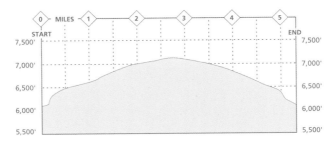

Rattlesnake Gulch

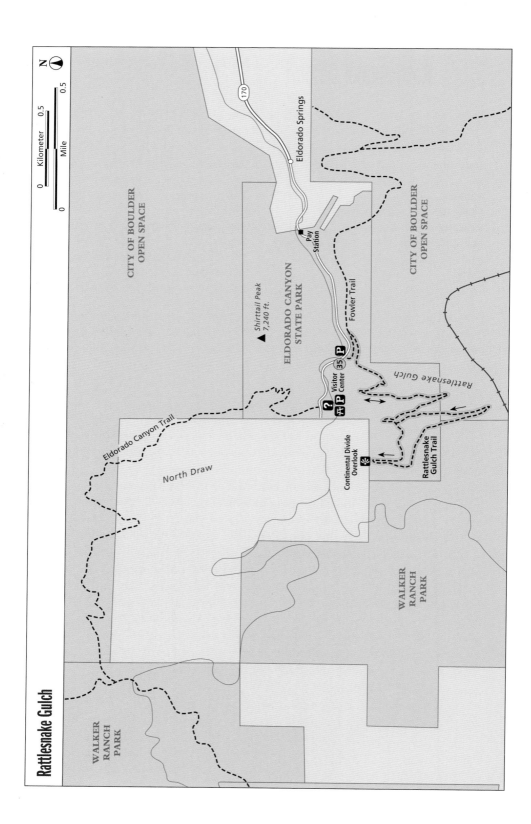

The trail switchbacks up the hill, and then reaches an open area, with views to the north, east, and west. Travel a short distance and reach the remains of the old Crags Hotel, built in the early 1900s. The hotel was reached via train or tramway, and was in operation for four years before burning down. Only the foundation of the hotel remains to tell the tale of a once popular getaway for tourists.

Pass the remains and travel through a forest of Douglas firs and ponderosa pines. At around the 2.3-mile mark the trail splits: This is the start of the loop portion of the hike. Go left and up the narrow trail into the pines. The trail curves back east and then meets with the main trail at around the 2.7-mile mark. Go left and begin a steep descent back down Rattlesnake Gulch.

The author on an early morning hike on this spectacular trail

On the way back to the road, if you have the time, follow the Fowler Trail to the east and around the backside of the Bastille. Interpretive signs are located along the trail, as are benches where you can take a break and look at the rock climbers scaling the vertical walls. A climber's trail goes down the west side of the Bastille, and will drop you on the road a short distance from the parking area. Go right, back to the parking area.

Miles and Directions

0.0 Start from the parking area; walking up the road pass several large rock walls.

0.6 Arrive at the Fowler Trail on the left.

0.8 Go right on the Rattlesnake Gulch Trail.

2.0 Arrive at the old hotel ruins and the start of the upper loop.

2.7 Go left ending the upper loop.

4.7 Arrive back at the Fowler Trail.

5.3 Arrive back at the parking area.

36 Eldorado Canyon Trail

This beautiful hike leads along towering rock walls. The trail travels up a south- and west-facing hillside through North Draw, with spectacular views of the Indian Peaks, the Continental Divide, Denver, and towering, sheer rock walls.

Start: From the parking area, walk north up steps and cross the road to the start of the signed trail.
Distance: 5.8 miles out and back
Hiking time: About 2.5 to 3.5 hours
Difficulty: Moderate
Trail surface: Smooth in parts, extremely rocky in others

Seasons: Year-round
Other trail users: Equestrians
Canine compatibility: Dogs must be on leash
Maps: USGS Boulder County; Colorado State Parks/Eldorado Canyon State Park map
Trail contact: Colorado State Parks; (303) 866-3437; www.parks.state.co.us

Finding the trailhead: From the intersection of Broadway and Baseline in Boulder, travel south on Broadway (CO 93) to CO 170. Go right on CO 170 for 4.4 miles to the entrance/fee station and parking area for Eldorado Canyon State Park. Pay the day-use fee and follow the dirt road up to the ranger station, parking area, and trailhead. GPS: N39 55.4927' / W105 17.3729'

The Hike

From the parking area at the ranger station, cross the road and access the Eldorado Canyon Trailhead. Begin a steep climb up into North Draw on the Eldorado Canyon Trail. Much work has been done on the lower section of the trail to eliminate cutting switchbacks, so stay on the main trail.

You gain altitude quickly as the trail climbs up into North Draw. Great views open to the north, of Shirt Tail Peak and towering rock walls that are popular with rock climbers from around the world. Eldorado Canyon has been a popular spot for rock climbers since the 1950s, and has been at the forefront of Colorado rock climbing since then.

At around the 0.4-mile mark, the trail climbs through a series of steep switchbacks across a steep hillside. At the top of the switchbacks a climbers' trail on the right leads to the Rincon Wall. Continue straight on the Eldorado Canyon Trail.

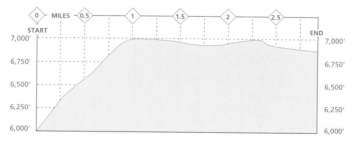

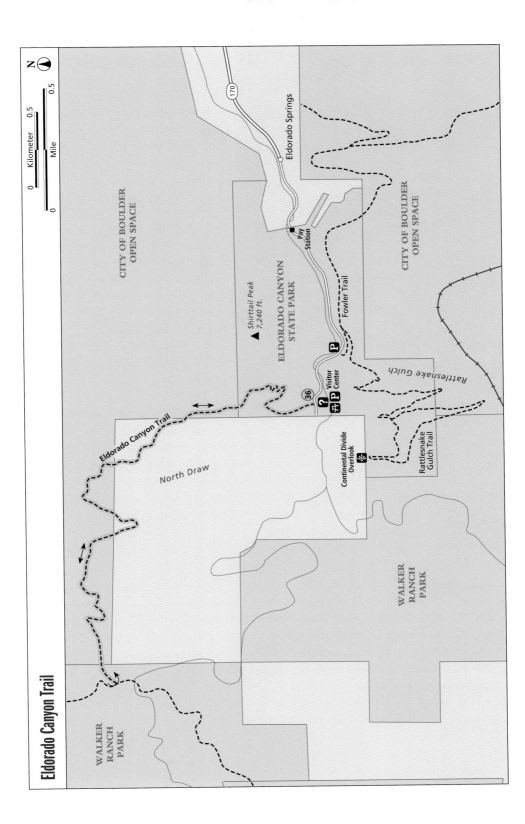

Eldorado Canyon Trail

Summer hiking at its best on the lower section of the trail

The trail becomes level and views open to the west, onto the Indian Peaks and the Continental Divide. Cacti, yuccas, and other sun-loving plants grow on the west-facing hillside, which becomes quite colorful with blooming flowers and cacti during the late spring and early summer months.

At around the 1.3-mile mark the trail climbs five steep switchbacks and enters into a dense pine forest. Large, colorful boulders line the trail and a small spring seeps out from one of the boulders, just to the right of the trail. The trail curves to the west and crosses over a small seasonal drainage via a wood footbridge.

Beyond the footbridge, the trail begin a modest climb up through the pines to an open meadow filled with yuccas and small ponderosas, with great views to the east, south, and west. South Boulder Peak (8,549 feet) looms high above to the northeast, and the trail cuts a straight line across the meadow and climbs up a short, rocky section, gaining a small ridge and high point with great views south to Eldorado Mountain.

At around the 2.9-mile mark, the trail begins to drop and goes right, down into Walker Ranch Open Space. This is the turnaround point of this hike. Feel free to drop down to Walker Ranch and South Boulder Creek for more mileage and views. Otherwise, retrace your steps to the trailhead.

Miles and Directions

0.0 Start by heading up into North Draw on the Eldorado Canyon Trail.

0.5 A climbers' trail to Rincon Wall goes right.

1.3 Arrive at a series of steep switchbacks.

2.9 Arrive at the turnaround point and great views to the west.

5.8 Arrive back at the trailhead.

Denver:
Foothills and Mountains

37 Barr Lake State Park

A beautiful, easy hike along the shoreline of Barr Lake offers great views of the Indian Peaks and Rocky Mountain National Park. You can see for a hundred miles to the north and south along the Front Range. This hike offers a different experience than most hikes along the Front Range and is a welcome relief from the steep trails along the foothills and the mountains. This is one of the best spots along the Front Range for wildlife viewing, and there are several spots along the trail where you can stop and look for the many species of birds and mammals that call this special place home. This is a great hike for the whole family to get out and enjoy some excellent hiking in a wonderful wildlife area.

Start: From the Barr Lake Nature Center, travel over the Denver and Hudson Canal via a footbridge.
Distance: 9.2-mile loop
Hiking time: About 3 to 5 hours
Difficulty: Moderate to strenuous
Trail surface: Smooth doubletrack trail

Seasons: Year-round
Other trail users: Mountain bikers and equestrians
Canine compatibility: Dogs must be on leash
Maps: Barr Lake State Park map
Trail contact: Colorado State Parks; (303) 866-3437; www.parks.state.co.us

Finding the trailhead: From Denver, travel north on I-76 to Bromley Lane (exit 22). Go right on Bromley for 1 mile to Picadilly Road, then go right on Picadilly Road for 1.7 miles to the park entrance. The hike starts at the nature center. GPS: N39 56.5072' / W104 44.5073'

The Hike

From the Barr Lake Nature Center travel over the Denver and Hudson Canal via a footbridge. Go left, with the canal on your left and the lake on the right. Follow the Niedrach Nature Trail on the right toward the lake. The trail will access the shoreline of the lake via a boardwalk. Large cottonwoods stand near the lake and offer welcome shade during the summer months. The nature trail soon joins the main trail and heads west, with great views of the Front Range. Several observation stations are situated in small meadows and can be accessed via side trails; they provide a great opportunity to view the wildlife near the lake.

At the 1.4-mile mark the Gazebo Trail shoots off to the right to a large observation deck. Take the trail if you like. A telescope can be used to sight the many migratory birds that call this area home. Bald eagles nest in the winter

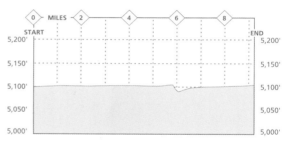

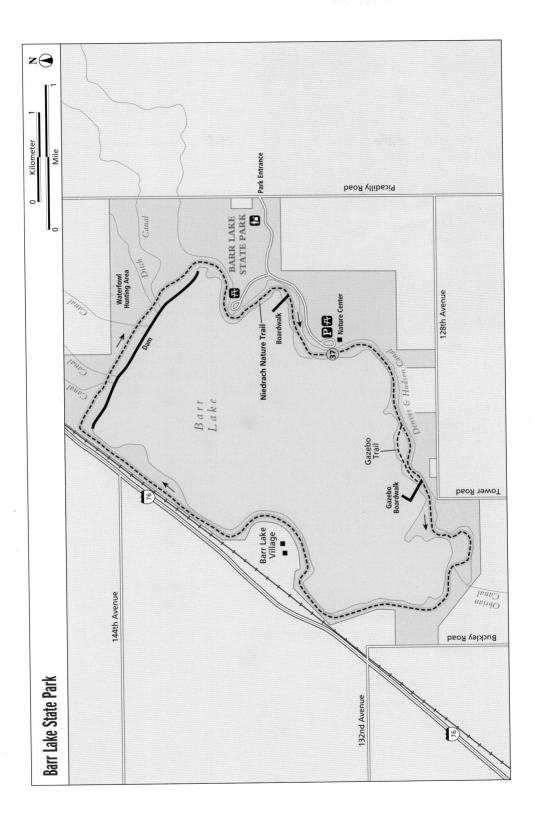

Barr Lake State Park

A resident at Barr Lake

months at Barr Lake and can be seen in the large cottonwoods along the shore. Beautiful meadows and cattail marshes line the lake past the Gazebo Trail, and offer a different beauty not usually seen along the Front Range.

At around the 2.5-mile mark the trail pulls away from the canal and heads north to the eagle nesting area. At the 2.9-mile mark, on the side of the trail, a makeshift tube/pipe allows hikers to look into an eagle's nest. Take a few minutes to locate the large nest high above the lake in a large cottonwood. Keep an eye out for these beautiful birds during the winter months.

Most hikers turn around at this point and retrace their route back to the Barr Lake nature center. Feel free to do so, but it is worth the effort to complete the loop.

At around the 4.9-mile mark, the trail parallels railroad tracks for a short distance. Noise from the nearby interstate is quite a contrast to the solitude of the previous miles. Before long the trail meets the north end of the dam and follows a service road past several hunting blinds off to the left, in the open fields. This area is popular with hunters during the fall months, so use caution when traveling through this section.

At around the 7.8-mile mark, the trail follows the canal to the boat ramp access and picnic area. Cross over the road and head south back to the trailhead.

Bring a pair of binoculars, water, and a snack and enjoy this beautiful riparian area.

Miles and Directions

0.0 Start by crossing the Denver and Hudson Canal.

1.4 Arrive at a junction with the Gazebo Trail.

2.9 Looks for an eagle's nest in the cottonwood trees.

4.9 Railroad tracks on the left.

5.8 Arrive at a small dam.

7.9 Arrive at the boat ramp and picnic area.

9.2 Arrive back at the trailhead.

38 Golden Gate State Park

A beautiful and seldom-visited state park is located 25 miles west of Denver. The main attractions on this hike are great vistas, wildflowers, colorful aspens in the fall, an old homestead, fishing, and rugged hiking if you do the loop.

Start: From the trailhead, go left up the signed Burro Trail.
Distance: 8.2-mile loop
Hiking time: About 3.5 to 5 hours
Difficulty: Moderate to strenuous
Trail surface: Rocky to smooth
Seasons: Year-round

Other trail users: Mountain bikers and equestrians
Canine compatibility: Dogs must be on leash
Map: Golden Gate State Park map
Trail contact: Colorado State Parks; (303) 866-3437; www.parks.state.co.us

Finding the trailhead: From the intersection of US 6 and CO 93 near Golden, drive 1.4 miles north on CO 93 and turn left on Golden Gate Canyon Road. Go 12.3 miles on Golden Gate Canyon Road to the visitor center and entrance to Golden Gate State Park. Turn right on Ralston Creek Road and go 1.9 miles to the Bridge Creek Trailhead and parking lot. GPS: N39 51.0633' / W105 25.0572'

The Hike

From the trailhead, go left up the Burro Trail, climbing steeply to a ridge. At the 0.6-mile mark, go left on the Mountain Lion Trail and begin a gradual descent into Forgotten Valley. Forgotten Valley has a pond and old settlement on the left. The pond is stocked with fish, so feel free to drop a line if you brought a rod. If you have the family along, this is a great destination in itself and a great spot to bring the kids. Pack a picnic lunch and hang around the pond for pure family fun.

For the hard-core hikers this is a great loop around the park, with lots of steep and rocky hiking. If you are not up to the task at hand, the Forgotten Valley pond is a great spot to turn around and head back to the trailhead.

At around the 1.5-mile mark, you will come to a junction with the Buffalo Trail. Continue straight on the Mountain Lion Trail, and begin a steep climb up several switchbacks, heading toward Windy Peak (9,141 feet). At around the 2.3-mile mark you arrive at a notch, with great views back to the east. Travel through a dense pine forest and come to a junction with the Burro Trail. Go left on the Mountain Lion Trail and drop down several rocky switchbacks to Deer Creek. Time to get your feet wet: For the next 2 miles the trail crosses Deer Creek several times. During the summer months wildflowers grow profusely in the moist soil along the creek. Old tree bridges help with negotiating the wet terrain, but I found keeping my feet dry almost impossible. Aspens and pine trees cling to the steep hillsides flanking the creek, and in the fall the golden aspens light up the dark, narrow hillsides.

Golden Gate State Park

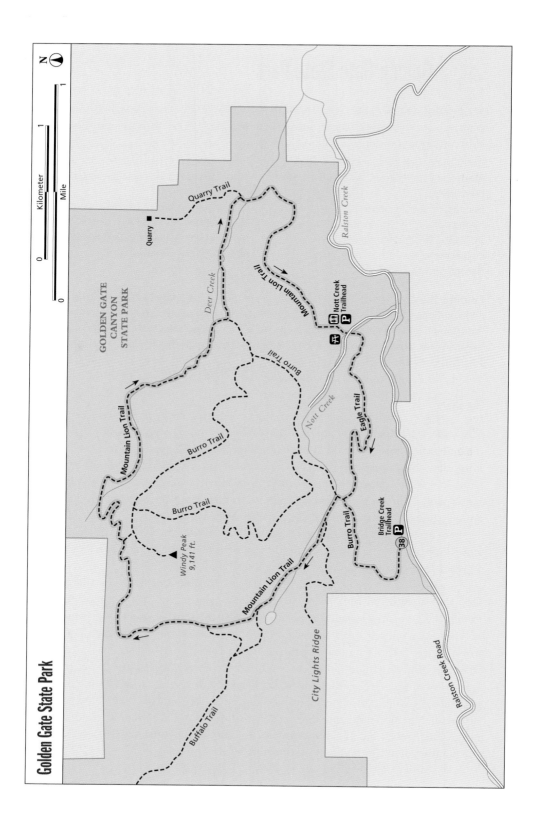

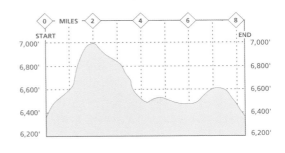

The Mountain Lion Trail breaks out into an open meadow at around the 4.5-mile mark and you quickly arrive at the junction with the Quarry Trail. Go right on the Mountain Lion Trail, crossing a bridge and climbing gently to a trail junction. At the 5.4-mile mark, go right and down to the Nott Creek Trailhead and restrooms. Go right at the restrooms and access the Eagle Trail. The Eagle Trail drops down, then climbs steeply up several switchbacks, then drops again to the Burro Trail. At the trail junction go left on the Burro Trail, heading back to the trailhead and your car.

The history of Golden Gate State Park is almost as colorful as the changing aspens. John Frazer homesteaded in what is now the park and was known to be somewhat of an eccentric. Anders Tallman, a Swedish immigrant, settled what is now Forgotten Valley. He chose this area for its natural beauty and a resemblance to his native homeland. The farmers in the area also made bootleg whisky at harvest time. As many as seventeen stills were in operation during the early 1900s, and the farmers would make daily runs to Denver and Central City to make sure the folks in those Western towns enjoyed the fruits of their harvest.

Miles and Directions

0.0 Start by climbing up the Burro Trail.

0.6 Go left on the Mountain Lion Trail.

1.5 Arrive at a junction with the Buffalo Trail.

2.5 Arrive at a junction with the Burro Trail.

4.7 Arrive at a junction with Quarry Trail.

5.4 Arrive at the Nott Creek Trailhead.

5.9 Arrive at the Eagle Trail junction.

7.7 Arrive at the Burro Trail junction.

8.2 Arrive back at the trailhead and parking area.

39 White Ranch Open Space

A nice hike up Belcher Hill in the White Ranch Open Space Park presents great views east to Denver and north along the foothills.

Start: From the parking area, walk north past the kiosk and then through a gate to the start of the trail.
Distance: 5.1-mile loop
Hiking time: About 2 to 3.5 hours
Difficulty: Moderate
Trail surface: Well maintained; some steep and rocky sections
Seasons: Year-round; can be snow-packed in the winter months

Other trail users: Mountain bikers and equestrians
Canine compatibility: Dogs must be on leash
Maps: Jefferson County White Ranch Open Space Park map
Trail contact: Jefferson County Open Space; (303) 271-5925; http://jeffco.us/openspace/index.htm

Finding the trailhead: From the intersection of US 6 and CO 93 in Golden, drive 3.4 miles north on CO 93, and go left on 56th Avenue. Follow the signs to the large open space parking area on the right. GPS: N39 47.5656' / W105 14.5440'

The Hike

Pass through the gate and drop down a small hill with great views to the north. On Belcher Hill Trail, go left through a rocky and sometime wet section—with great wildflowers in the summer months—to a bridge. Cross the bridge and then begin an extended climb up Belcher Hill, with spectacular views east to Denver and the plains.

Pass a junction with the Longhorn Trail and continue climbing up the steep rocky Belcher Hill Trail to a junction with the Mustang Trail. Go right on the Longhorn Trail, and drop steeply to a junction with the Longhorn Trail. Go right on the Longhorn Trail and continue for a short distance to a junction with the Belcher Hill Trail. From here, retrace your route back down the Belcher Hill Trail to the parking area.

Caution: This is a popular trail with other users. Be courteous and share the trail.

Miles and Directions

0.0 Go through the gate and drop down a small hill. The Belcher Hill trail cuts through a rock garden, then crosses a bridge, and then climbs up the obvious steep hill.

1.8 The Longhorn Trail goes right; continue straight on Belcher Hill Trail.

2.5 Reach the Mustang Trail on the right. Go right and follow the Mustang Trail down to a junction with Longhorn Trail.

3.1 Go right on the Longhorn Trail.

3.3 Go left on the Belcher Hill Trail.

5.1 Arrive back at the trailhead and parking area.

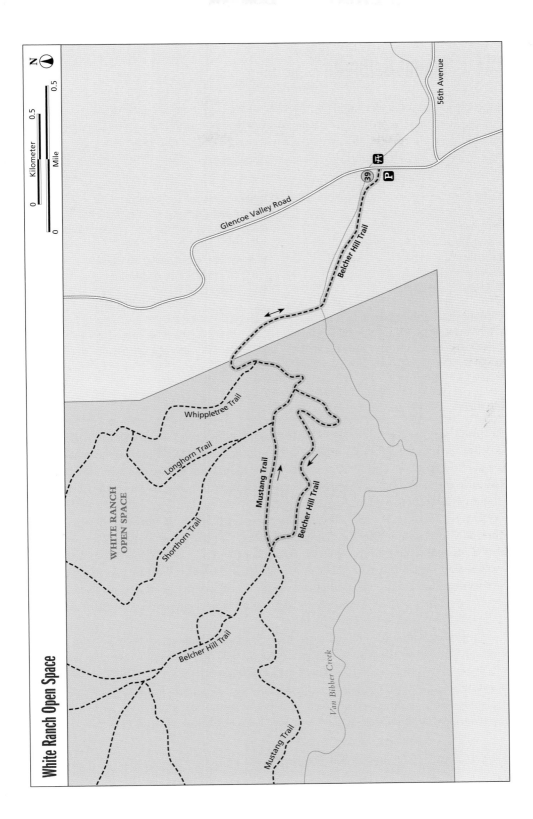

White Ranch Open Space

40 Mount Galbraith

A beautiful hike up and around Mount Galbraith (7,163 feet) on a trail in one of the newest Jefferson County Open Space parks. There are beautiful vistas in all directions. Wildflowers, yuccas, cacti, cedar, ponderosas, juniper, and lodgepole pines line the trail, which travels through several deep-cut gulches up to Mount Galbraith.

Start: From the parking area, walk west to the signed Cedar Gulch Trail just past the kiosk.
Distance: 4.0-mile loop
Hiking time: About 2 to 3.5 hours
Difficulty: Moderate
Trail surface: Rocky in sections
Seasons: Year-round

Other trail users: Equestrians
Canine compatibility: Dogs must be on leash
Maps: Jefferson County Open Space/Mount Galbraith map
Trail contact: Jefferson County Open Space; (303) 271-5925; http://jeffco.us/open space/index.htm

Finding the trailhead: From Denver, travel west on US 6 to Golden and the junction with CO 93. Turn right on CO 93 and travel 2 miles north to Golden Gate Canyon Road. Turn left on Golden Gate Canyon Road and travel 1.3 miles to the Mount Galbraith Trailhead and parking area on the left. GPS: N39 46.2523' / W105 15.1459'

The Hike

From the parking area, access the Cedar Gulch Trail near the kiosk and cross over a small seasonal creek. The trail heads west along the creek and begins to climb along the north side of a steep hill. It then cuts across the hillside and passes by a rock wall on the right at the 0.3-mile mark. Beautiful cedar trees cling to the steep hillside, along with yuccas and mahogany oak.

Reach a small rocky saddle at the 0.5-mile mark, with great views to the east. At the saddle look to the right of the trail and along the ground at all the quartz rocks. You are standing on a barely exposed rock dike.

The trail makes a sharp right at the saddle, and cuts across the east side of a steep hill. Cedar, juniper, and ponderosa trees line the trail, along with yuccas and sun-loving pricklypear cacti. Climb a steady grade and reach the junction with the Mount Galbraith Loop Trail at the 1.3-mile mark.

Turn right on the Mount Galbraith Loop Trail and climb across a steep open hill, with good views to the east, to a saddle. Reach the saddle and enjoy open views to the north and west. The trail goes left and climbs a series of rock steps, entering a beautiful stand of ponderosas and lodgepole pines. It is narrow and rocky, with steep drop-offs to the right. The path follows a line through the rocks and climbs to an open meadow with expansive views south to Lookout Mountain and west to Mount

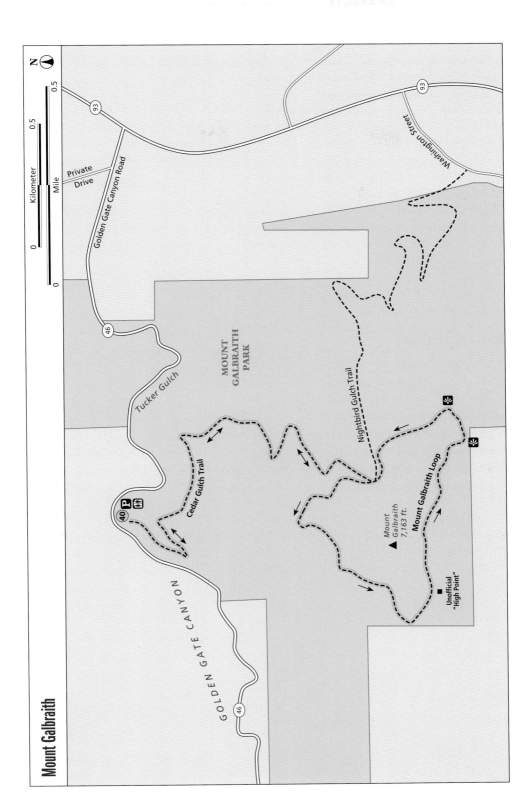

Mount Galbraith

Evans and the Continental Divide. The meadow is filled with beautiful tall grasses and ponderosas, and is a great place to stop and enjoy the views.

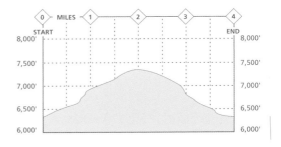

Follow rock cairns through a rocky area and reach the halfway and high point of the hike. Indian Gulch, Clear Creek, and Clear Creek Canyon are to the south, and a thousand feet below you. The trail drops at a gentle grade and cuts through a rocky section, with an overlook on the right. Head to the north and reach a second overlook in a small, open meadow, with stunted ponderosas along both sides of the trail. Enjoy great views, following the trail along the east side of Mount Galbraith and back to the Cedar Gulch Trail. Turn right on the Cedar Gulch Trail, enjoying open views to the east and north, and retrace your route back to the trailhead.

Miles and Directions

0.0   Start on the Cedar Gulch Trail.

0.5   Reach a saddle and overlook with great views to the north.

1.3   Junction with the Mount Galbraith Loop Trail.

1.6   Climb up a series of rock steps.

2.1   Reach an overlook with great views.

2.3   Reach a second overlook with great views.

2.7   Back at the Cedar Gulch Trail.

4.0   Arrive back at the trailhead.

41 Chimney Gulch

A steep hike leads into and up Chimney Gulch, located a mile from downtown Golden. Excellent views of Denver, the plains, and up Clear Creek Canyon can be seen from Windy Saddle. The trail climbs through Chimney Gulch and along steep hillsides covered with wildflowers, cacti, yuccas, and mixed pine forests. This is a year-round trail that is especially beautiful during the early summer months.

Start: From the parking area, follow the Chimney Gulch Trail north across a small, open meadow.
Distance: 7.0 miles out and back
Hiking time: About 3 to 4 hours
Difficulty: Moderate
Trail surface: Smooth on the lower section, rocky above Windy Saddle
Seasons: Year-round

Other trail users: Mountain bikers and equestrians
Canine compatibility: Dogs permitted
Maps: Jefferson County Open Space/Lookout Mountain map
Trail contact: Jefferson County Open Space; (303) 271-5925; http://jeffco.us/open space/index.htm

Finding the trailhead: From Denver, travel west on US 6 to its junction with CO 93 in Golden. Travel south on US 6 for 0.5 mile to a parking area on the right. The parking area is located just past a large TOWN OF GOLDEN sign and at a wind sock (used by paragliders). The hike starts here. GPS: N39 45.0011' / W105 13.4377'

The Hike

From the parking area, follow the Chimney Gulch Trail north across a small, open meadow. Watch out for landing paragliders. When you reach a dirt road, go left up the road to a cement ditch. Walk over the ditch and head right and up the Chimney Gulch Trail with beautiful yuccas along both sides.

Follow the trail through a short, rocky section to the crest of a small hill and a trail junction. Go left (southwest) up the Chimney Gulch Trail and into Chimney Gulch. The trail hugs the side of the gulch, with nice-looking cottonwoods to the left. Follow a series of steep switchbacks up to a private driveway. At the driveway turn left, following the trail markers. Make a quick right onto a narrow trail, passing a house on the left.

After 0.9 mile of fairly steep hiking, you arrive at Lookout Mountain Road. Cross Lookout Mountain Road to the trail on the other side. Watch out for car traffic. Follow the trail up and into Chimney Gulch, past several rocky sections.

This section of the trail hugs the north side of the gulch and is filled with blooming wildflowers and yuccas during the early summer months. At around the 1.6-mile mark the trail becomes quite narrow, passing through a stand of young cottonwood trees. The trail follows the contour of the steep hill and stays close to a seasonal creek down and to the left.

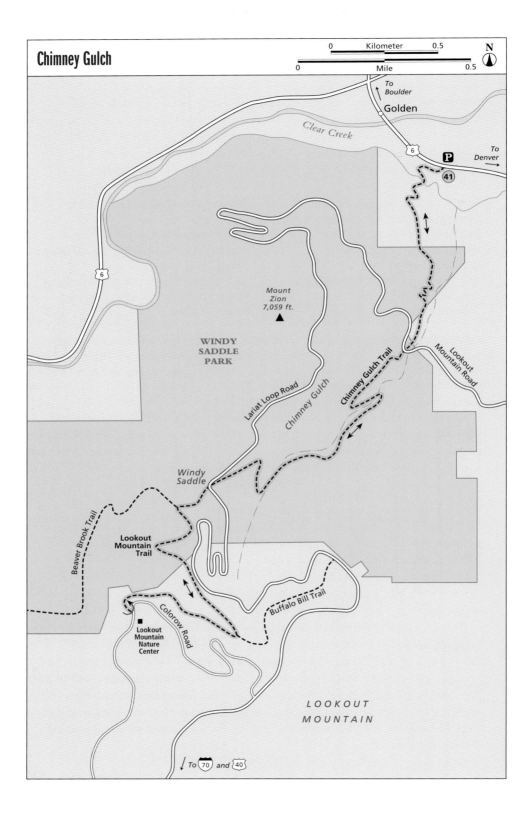

Chimney Gulch

Kilometer

0   0.5

0   Mile   0.5

N

To Boulder

Golden

Clear Creek

6

To Denver

P

41

Mount Zion 7,059 ft.

WINDY SADDLE PARK

6

Lariat Loop Road

Chimney Gulch

Chimney Gulch Trail

Lookout Mountain Road

Windy Saddle

Beaver Brook Trail

Lookout Mountain Trail

Buffalo Bill Trail

Colorow Road

Lookout Mountain Nature Center

LOOKOUT MOUNTAIN

To 70 and 40

Arrive at a wood footbridge, where the trail cuts sharply back to the east. There are views of Golden, Table Mountain, Denver, tract houses, and the sprawling Coors Brewery.

The trail climbs through a beautiful forest of juniper, Douglas firs, and ponderosa pines. Reach a second footbridge and climb to the north, away from Chimney Gulch, to Lookout Mountain Road at the 2.4-mile mark. This is a good spot to take a short rest and enjoy the views east to Denver and west up Clear Creek Canyon.

Go left up Lookout Mountain Road for a very short distance to the Lookout Mountain/Beaver Brook Trail on the right. Follow the trail up into the pines, with excellent views to the west, to where the trails split at the 2.6-mile mark. The Beaver Brook Trail heads north (right) and the Lookout Mountain Trail goes west (left). Follow the Lookout Mountain Trail up through a shady area of tall pines to an overlook at the 2.9-mile mark.

Stop at the lookout and enjoy views to the west. The trail climbs up through the pines at a gentle grade and reaches Colorow Road and the Lookout Mountain Nature Center at the 3.5-mile mark. This is the turnaround point for this hike. Retrace your steps to the trailhead.

Feel free to visit the Lookout Mountain Nature Center, located near the Boettcher Mansion. The nature center is a great place to bring the family and learn about the ecology, geology, and animal life in the area. The center runs year-round programs and is open every day except Mon from 10 a.m. to 4 p.m. Call (303) 526-0594 for more information.

Miles and Directions

0.0   Start from the parking area and head west through an open field.

0.7   Reach a private driveway.

0.9   Cross over Lookout Mountain Road.

1.8   Cross over a wood bridge.

2.2   Cross over a second wood bridge.

2.4   Arrive at Lookout Mountain Road and Windy Saddle.

2.6   Arrive at a junction with Beaver Brook Trail.

3.5   Colorow Road and Lookout Mountain Nature Center.

7.0   Arrive back at the trailhead.

42 Apex Park

Situated below Lookout Mountain, and surrounded by ever-increasing urban sprawl, lies this beautiful piece of open space. Apex Park is a quick getaway into a beautiful deep gulch that offers hikers great views, beautiful wildflowers, cacti, yuccas, and a pine forest—all a mere 15 miles from downtown Denver.

Start: From the parking area, head west to the signed Apex Trail.
Distance: 5.3-mile loop
Hiking time: About 2 to 3 hours
Difficulty: Moderate
Trail surface: Rocky in sections
Seasons: Year-round
Other trail users: Mountain bikers and equestrians

Canine compatibility: Dogs must be on leash or voice control
Maps: Jefferson County Open Space/Apex Park map
Trail contact: Jefferson County Open Space; (303) 271-5925; http://jeffco.us/open space/index.htm

Finding the trailhead: From Denver, go west on I-70 to the Morrison exit (US 40). Go 1 mile east on US 40 to just past the Heritage Square entrance, and make a left. Make another quick left into the Apex Park east parking lot, just before the Golden Fire Station No. 4. GPS: N39 42.5679' / W105 12.4095'

The Hike

Once the site of the thriving town of Apex and a toll road to the gold mines of Central City and Blackhawk, Apex Open Space Park is a beautiful oasis in an area of ever-increasing urban sprawl.

From the parking area, head west along a seasonal creek amid nice cottonwoods. Cross over a bridge and follow the wide Apex Trail through a large lot up to the start of the gulch and a toll road sign. The trail you now travel was once used by miners and supply wagons going to and from the gold mines near Blackhawk and Central City.

Follow the trail into the gulch along the creek. The trail becomes somewhat rocky, and climbs to a junction with Pick 'n' Sledge Trail. Continue straight on the

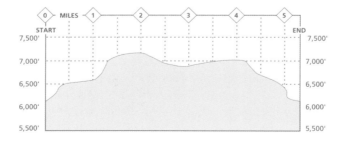

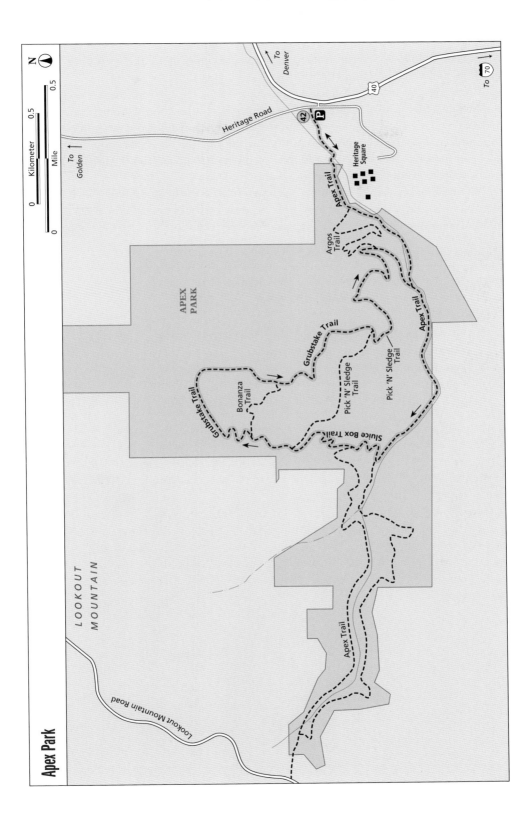

Apex Park

Apex Trail. Wildflowers, scrub oak, cacti, and yuccas grow along this section of the gulch, as well as the occasional cottonwood.

Continue west up the gulch to the Sluicebox Trail at the 1.4-mile mark. Go right on the Sluicebox Trail and climb eleven switchbacks to a junction with the Bonanza and Grubstake Trails. Continue straight on the Grubstake Trail and enter a forest of lodgepole and ponderosa pines. Pleasant hiking through the pines takes you through an open meadow and along the east side of Indian Mountain. Enjoy views to the north and east while traversing the mountain.

The trail makes a steep drop down an open hillside to the Apex Trail. The hill is covered in yuccas and cacti, and uses three steep switchbacks to reach the Apex Trail and the creek. Go left on the Apex Trail, and retrace your route back to the trailhead.

Miles and Directions

0.0 Start from the parking area and head north on the marked Apex Trail.

0.7 Arrive at a junction with the Pick 'n' Sledge Trail.

1.4 Sluice Box Trail.

1.9 Arrive at a junction with the Bonanza Trail and Grubstake Trail junction.

4.6 Arrive back at the Apex Trail. Retrace your steps.

5.3 Arrive back at the trailhead.

43 Beaver Brook Trail

This is a nice hike in the trees high above Clear Creek and Clear Creek Canyon. The Beaver Brook Trail runs in an east-to-west direction for 7 miles. Feel free to extend your mileage and hike as far as you like. Beautiful views reach up and down Clear Creek Canyon and west to the Continental Divide.

Start: From the parking area at Windy Saddle, pass the kiosk and access the Lookout Mountain Trail.
Distance: 3.2 miles out and back
Hiking time: About 2 to 3 hours
Difficulty: Easy to moderate
Trail surface: Extremely rocky in sections
Seasons: Year-round

Other trail users: None
Canine compatibility: Dogs permitted
Maps: Denver Mountain Parks/Beaver Brook Trail map
Trail contact: Denver Mountain Parks; http://www.denvergov.org/parks/Welcome/tabid/433973/Default.aspx

Finding the trailhead: From Denver, travel west on US 6 to Golden. Go left (west) on Lookout Mountain Road/Lariat Loop for 4.4 miles to Windy Saddle, the trailhead, and the parking area. GPS: N39 44.1243' / W105 14.4351'

The Hike

From the parking area at Windy Saddle, pass the kiosk and access the Lookout Mountain Trail. Follow the Lookout Mountain Trail into the trees and up to a junction with the Beaver Brook Trail. At the junction, go right on the Beaver Brook Trail.

Follow the trail into the trees and reach a cluster of boulders. Stay to the left and uphill side of the boulders. The trail cuts through two large boulders, then rolls to a series of rocky sections. Scramble through the boulders and reach a narrow gully with a seasonal stream. A tall rock cliff looms above the trail, and the steep slope drops to Clear Creek on the right.

Continue on the narrow path and cut across a slide area. The trail begins to descend into the woods, passing several rocky sections, and enters an open area filled with tall grasses and views to the east, down to Clear Creek and US 6.

At around the 1.3-mile mark, the trail crosses a seasonal stream and travels through a dense pine forest to an open meadow. Right of the trail is a flat, rocky ledge that offers great views of Clear Creek Canyon. Continue on if you have the time; this hike ends here. Retrace your route back to Windy Saddle.

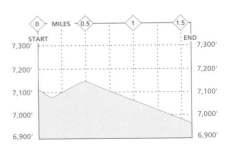

Beaver Brook Trail

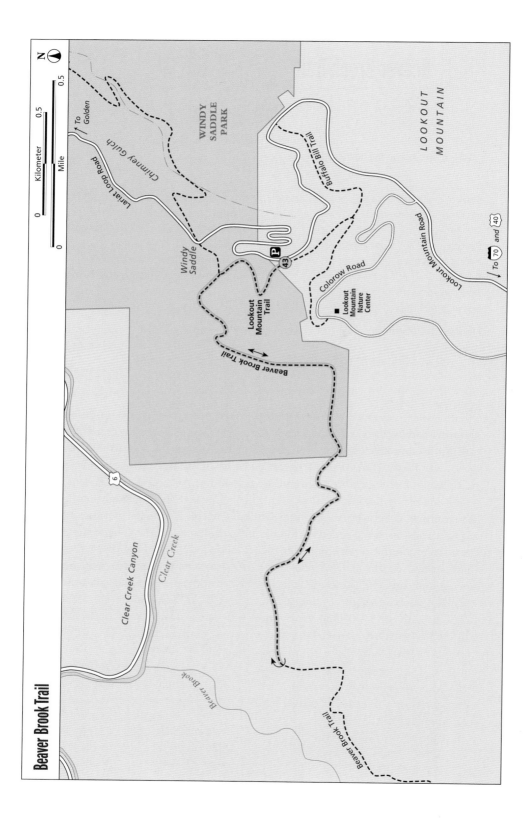

Miles and Directions

0.0 Start at Windy Saddle, following the Lookout Mountain Trail.

0.1 At the junction with the Beaver Brook Trail, go right on Beaver Brook.

0.7 Seasonal stream crossing.

1.6 Open meadow and turnaround point. Retrace your steps.

3.2 Arrive back at the trailhead.

44 Dakota Ridge Trail

Take a trip back into time. Dinosaurs roamed this land millions of years ago, and this hike takes you to the fossilized remains and footprints of these prehistoric animals via the Dakota Ridge Trail and Rooney Road.

Start: From the parking area, cross CO 26 and access the fire road on the east side of the highway.
Distance: 4.2 miles out and back
Hiking time: About 2 to 4 hours
Difficulty: Easy to moderate
Trail surface: Rocky
Seasons: Year-round

Other trail users: Mountain bikers and equestrians
Canine compatibility: Dogs must be on leash
Maps: Jefferson County Open Space/ Matthews-Winters Open Space Park map
Trail contact: Jefferson County Open Space; (303) 271-5925; http://jeffco.us/open space/index.htm

Finding the trailhead: From Denver, travel west on I-70 to the Morrison/Golden exit and CR 93. Travel west on CR 93 for 0.2 mile to the Matthews/Winters Open Space parking area on the right. Turn right into the parking lot. The hike starts here. GPS: N39 41.4020' / W105 12.1188'

The Hike

From the parking area, cross CO 26 and access the fire road on the east side of the highway. Pass through a gate and climb up to a trail marker at the 0.8-mile mark. Go right at the trail marker and climb along the crest of the ridge.

The Dakota Ridge Trail cuts through a forest of small juniper and ponderosa pines, and stays on the west side of the ridge. Reach a trail marker and the top of the ridge. The trail cuts to the east side of the ridge and drops on rocky tread into a small meadow. Wildflowers, cacti, and yuccas bloom in this picturesque little meadow in the late spring, along with meadow grass.

Follow the trail through the meadow and climb several wood steps through the pines to reach a high point on the ridge. The trail is extremely rocky through this section. Great views open to the east to Green Mountain and Denver, west to Mount Morrison, and south to Pikes Peak, towering in the southern skyline. The trail climbs

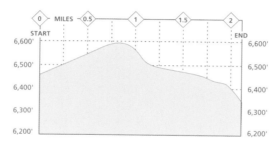

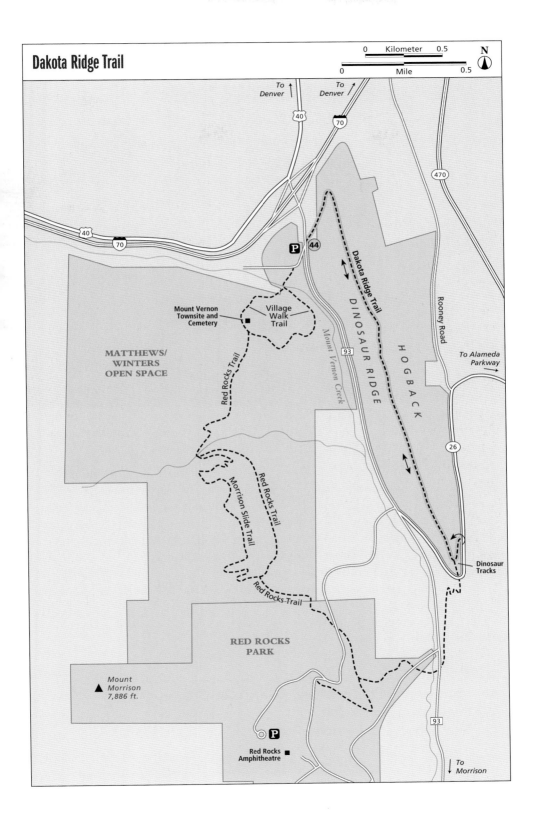

Dakota Ridge Trail

0 Kilometer 0.5
0 Mile 0.5

N

To Denver
To Denver
40
70
470

40
70

P 44

Mount Vernon Townsite and Cemetery

Village Walk Trail

MATTHEWS/ WINTERS OPEN SPACE

Red Rocks Trail

Mount Vernon Creek

93

Dakota Ridge Trail

DINOSAUR RIDGE

HOGBACK

Rooney Road

To Alameda Parkway

26

Morrison Slide Trail

Red Rocks Trail

Red Rocks Trail

Dinosaur Tracks

RED ROCKS PARK

Mount Morrison 7,886 ft.

P

Red Rocks Amphitheatre

93

To Morrison

Steep hiking to gain the ridge

a short distance and passes several sandstone outcrops on the right, coming extremely close to the edge of one of the cliffs. It then cuts to the left and drops steeply past several water bars to a trail junction. Go left at the junction, the Dakota Ridge Trail switchbacking on rocky tread down to Rooney Road. Go left on Rooney Road. past several interpretive signs on the left, to a large kiosk and dinosaur tracks. After exploring this area, hike back up Rooney Road past the Dakota Ridge Trail, and read the interpretive signs along Rooney Road to the west.

After enjoying your dinosaur tour, retrace your route back on the Dakota Ridge Trail to the trailhead.

This trail is extremely popular with hikers and mountain cyclists on weekends. Watch out for other trail users.

Miles and Directions

0.0   Start by crossing CO 26 and climbing the fire road toward the ridgetop.

0.8   The trail goes right up a steep hill.

2.1   Reach Rooney Road and the dinosaur tracks.

4.2   Arrive back at the trailhead.

45 Matthews/Winters Open Space

A beautiful hike leads up and through the foothills of Matthews/Winters Open Space Park. This hike takes you past the old cemetery and townsite of Mount Vernon, through open meadows filled with wildflowers with spectacular views to the north, east to Green Mountain and Dakota Ridge, and south to Pikes Peak.

Start: From the parking area, go down the steps past the kiosk to the signed Village Walk Trail.
Distance: 5.0-mile loop
Hiking time: About 2 to 3.5 hours
Difficulty: Easy to moderate
Trail surface: Rocky
Seasons: Year-round

Other trail users: Mountain bikers and equestrians
Canine compatibility: Dogs must be on leash
Maps: Jefferson County Open Space/ Matthews-Winters Open Space Park map
Trail contact: Jefferson County Open Space; (303) 271-5925; http://jeffco.us/open space/index.htm

Finding the trailhead: From Denver, travel west on I-70 to the Morrison/Golden exit and CR 93. Travel west on CR 93 for 0.2 mile to the Matthews/Winters Open Space parking area on the right. Turn right into the parking lot. The hike starts here. GPS: N39 41.4020' / W105 12.1683'

The Hike

From the parking area, go down the steps and pick up a park map at the kiosk. Follow the wide gravel path down past the restrooms and picnic area to a bridge. Cross the wood footbridge over Mount Vernon Creek and follow the Village Walk Trail up and to the right.

Mount Vernon Creek is quite picturesque and is surrounded by tall cottonwoods and willow bushes. The Village Walk Trail climbs a gentle grade through an open meadow filled with colorful wildflowers in the late spring and early summer months. The trail makes a sharp left at the top of the hill and climbs up to the Mount Vernon townsite.

Reach the townsite (not much left), cemetery, and a junction with the Red Rocks Trail at 0.4 mile. Check out the cemetery, then turn right on the Red Rocks Trail, following this beautiful trail in and out of several gulches and over two creek crossings

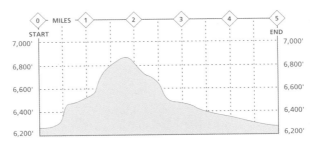

Hikers and dogs enjoying a beautiful winter hike

to a junction with the Morrison Slide Trail. Go up and to the right on the Morrison Slide Trail and climb steeply, passing several switchbacks with excellent views to the north and east.

The trail slices its way across the boulder-strewn hillside and makes a narrow passage through two large boulders to reach an overlook at the 1.8-mile mark. This is a good spot to take a break and enjoy the awesome views. Follow the trail up through a large open meadow, filled with prairie grasses, wildflowers, yuccas, and widely spaced juniper trees. Enjoy excellent views to the east and south. The trail hugs the edge of the meadow, with steep drop-offs to the left.

At the 2.3-mile mark the trail makes a steep drop down several rocky switchbacks, with beautiful views to the south and around towering red rock formations. Reach the Red Rocks Trail again at the 2.7-mile mark, and climb several wood steps to the crest of a hill and great views.

The Red Rocks Trail heads back to the north, clinging to the side of a steep hill through the juniper trees, and meets the Morrison Slide Trail at the 3.5-mile mark. Drop down, crossing the familiar creek, and follow the Red Rocks Trail back toward the Mount Vernon townsite.

Enjoy hiking with good views to the north and reach the Village Walk Trail at the 4.3-mile mark. Turn right on the Village Walk Trail and descend, passing rocks, trees, and tall shrubs, to reach Mount Vernon Creek. Follow the trail along the creek, under the canopy of tall cottonwoods, and reach the footbridge. Go right across the footbridge, past the restrooms and picnic area, and reach the end of the hike and the parking area.

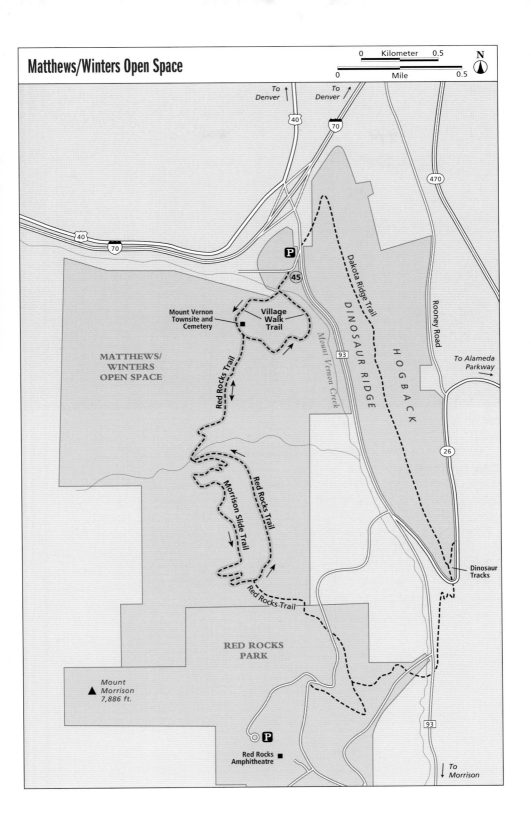

Matthews/Winters Open Space

0 — Kilometer — 0.5

0 — Mile — 0.5

N

To Denver

To Denver

40

70

470

40

70

40

70

P

45

Mount Vernon Townsite and Cemetery

Village Walk Trail

Dakota Ridge Trail

Mount Vernon Creek

93

DINOSAUR RIDGE

HOGBACK

Rooney Road

To Alameda Parkway

26

MATTHEWS/
WINTERS
OPEN SPACE

Red Rocks Trail

Morrison Slide Trail

Red Rocks Trail

Red Rocks Trail

Dinosaur Tracks

RED ROCKS
PARK

Mount
Morrison
7,886 ft.

P

Red Rocks
Amphitheatre

93

To Morrison

Matthew Winters Park

Miles and Directions

0.0 Start from the parking and head south across a small bridge on the marked Village Walk Trail.

0.4 Arrive at the Mount Vernon townsite and cemetery and a junction with the Red Rocks Trail. Go right on the Red Rocks Trail.

1.2 Arrive at a junction with the Morrison Slide Trail. Go right on the Morrison Slide Trail.

2.7 Arrive at a junction with the Red Rocks Trail. Go left on the Red Rocks Trail.

4.6 Arrrive back at the Village Walk Trail.

5.0 Arrive back at the parking area.

46 Mount Falcon Open Space

This nice hike features spectacular views of Red Rocks, the Continental Divide, and the plains. Expect to see wildlife, wildflowers, cacti, beautiful yuccas, and great views to the north, east, and west.

Start: From the parking area, drop down on the signed Castle Trail.
Distance: 9.5-mile loop
Hiking time: About 4 to 6 hours
Difficulty: Moderate to strenuous
Trail surface: Lower part of hike is rocky in sections; Parmalee Trail is rocky.
Seasons: Year-round

Other trail users: Mountain bikers and equestrians
Canine compatibility: Dogs must be on leash
Maps: Jefferson County Open Space/ Mount Falcon Park map
Trail contact: Jefferson County Open Space; (303) 271-5925; http://jeffco.us/open space/index.htm

Finding the trailhead: From Denver, travel west on I-70 to the Morrison/Golden exit and CR 93. Travel west on CR 93 for 4 miles to the town of Morrison. Go right on Main Street in Morrison, and then go left on CO 8 for 1.6 miles to Forest Avenue. Turn right on Forest Avenue and follow the signs for Mount Falcon Open Space, the trailhead, and the parking area. GPS: N39 38.4851' / W105 11.4711'

The Hike

From the parking area, drop down on the Castle Trail across a small gulch. Begin a steep climb through junipers, cacti, and yuccas, with good views to the east. At around the 0.7-mile mark the trail switchbacks to the north, with great views of Red Rocks. The trail turns back to the south and climbs several switchbacks. At around the 1.7-mile mark great views of Morrison and Denver appear. This is a good spot to take a short break.

The trail continues to climb into the pines, and becomes quite steep and rocky at the 2.3-mile mark. Power forward, and within a short distance reach a saddle and trail junction. The trail to the right leads to the Summer White House ruins and is 0.4-mile long. The trail going to the left is the Two-Dog Trail, which leads to an overlook and is 0.2-mile long. For this hike continue on the Castle Trail, climbing at a gentle grade to a junction with the Meadow Trail at the 3.4-mile mark. Wildflowers bloom in the early summer months along this section of the trail.

Stay to the right on the Castle Trail, dropping down a short hill and passing the Walker Home ruins on the right. At around the 3.7-mile mark, pass the restrooms on the right and make a quick left to the Parmalee Trail. The Parmalee Trail is 2 miles long, quite narrow, and crosses several seasonal creeks. It travels through ponderosas pines and hovers high above US 285, offering great views to the south and east. The

Mount Falcon Open Space

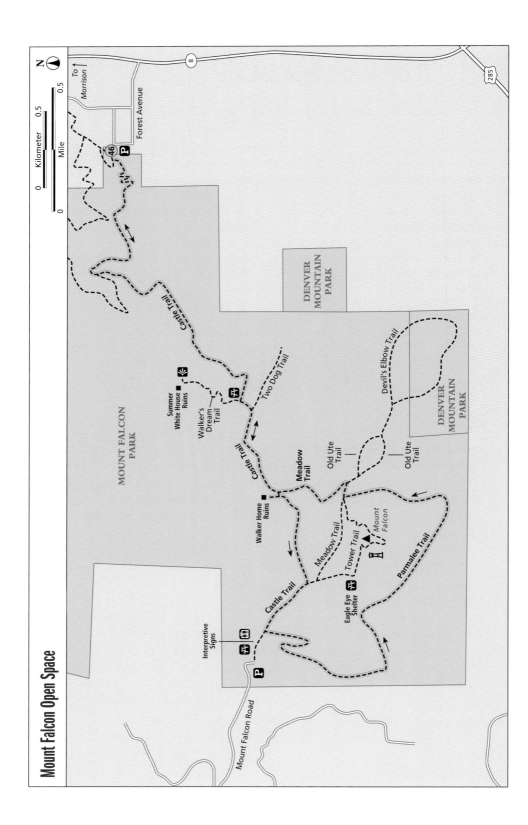

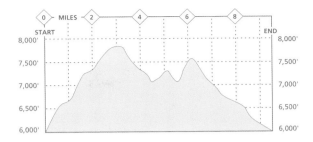

trail can be quite rocky in sections and is extremely narrow. Watch out for other trail users and yield the right-of-way to the uphill traveler.

At around the 6-mile mark, reach a second junction with the Meadow Trail. Go right on the Meadow Trail, and then make a quick left to stay on the Meadow Trail at a junction with the Old Ute Trail.

Follow the Meadow Trail across an open area. Reach the Castle Trail at the 6.4-mile mark and get ready for some fast downhill hiking. Go right on the Castle Trail and retrace your route back to the parking area.

Feel free to make this hike as long or short as you desire. Pick up a map at the trailhead and customize the hike to fit your time frame and ability.

Miles and Directions

0.0   Start by beginning the climb on the Castle Trail.

0.7   Great views north to Red Rocks.

2.7   Arrive at a junction with the Two-Dog Trail.

3.6   Arrive at a junction with the Meadow Trail.

3.7   Junction with the Parmalee Trail. Follow the Parmalee Trail.

6.4   Arrive back at the Castle Trail junction. Retrace your steps.

9.5   Arrive back at the trailhead.

47 Deer Creek Canyon Park

This nice hike through the beautiful foothills west of Denver features year-round access, marked trails, early summer wildflowers, and spectacular views from the summit of Plymouth Mountain (7,295 feet).

Start: From the parking area, access the well-marked Plymouth Creek Trail.
Distance: 5.6 miles out and back
Hiking time: About 2 to 3 hours
Difficulty: Moderate
Trail surface: Smooth on the lower section, rocky near the summit of Plymouth Mountain
Seasons: Year-round

Other trail users: Mountain bikers and equestrians
Canine compatibility: Dogs must be on leash
Maps: Jefferson County Open Space/Deer Creek Canyon Park map
Trail contact: Jefferson County Open Space; (303) 271-5925; http://jeffco.us/open space/index.htm

Finding the trailhead: From Denver, travel west on I-70 to C-470 east. Travel east on C-470 to the Wadsworth Boulevard exit (CO 121). Exit onto Wadsworth Boulevard and go south for 300 yards to Deer Creek Canyon Road. Turn west on Deer Creek Canyon Road and travel 4.9 miles to the park entrance. The hike starts near the restrooms. GPS: N39 32.3573' / W105 09.0713'

The Hike

From the parking area, access the well-marked Plymouth Creek Trail. Follow the Plymouth Creek Trail south on smooth tread. The trail stays level for a short distance, then begins a steady climb into the pines trees, with Plymouth Creek on your left. Be on the lookout for wildflowers that bloom in the early summer months along the banks and hillsides of the creek.

The trail becomes rough and rocky as you climb to a junction with the Meadowlark Trail on the right at the 1.2 mile mark. Continue straight on the Plymouth Creek Trail, and grind your way through a steep, rocky section of the trail. Slow things down a bit, catch your breath, and enjoy the beautiful hiking along Plymouth Creek.

At around the 1.9-mile mark, reach the junction with the Plymouth Mountain Trail. Turn left, and follow the Plymouth Mountain Trail into the pines. Look east for

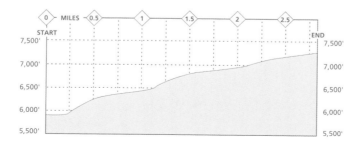

Deer Creek Canyon Park

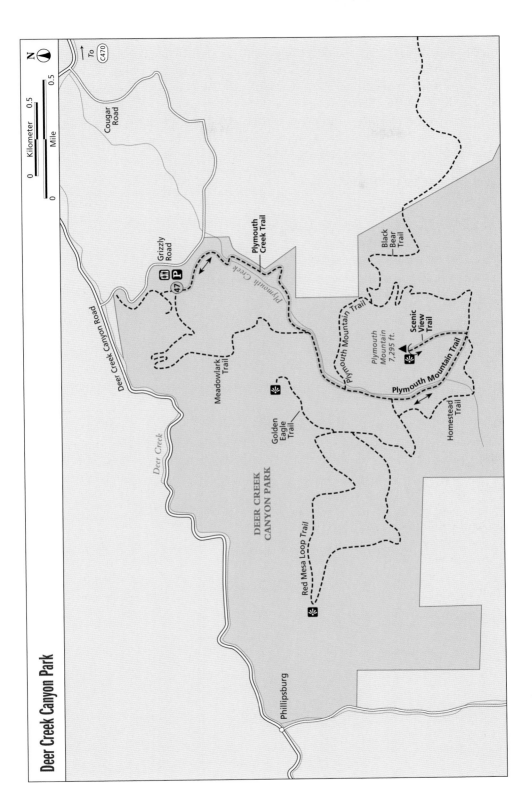

Deer Creek Canyon Park

To C470

Kilometer 0.5 0.5
Mile

N

Cougar Road

Grizzly Road

Plymouth Creek Trail

47

Deer Creek Canyon Road

Plymouth Creek

Meadowlark Trail

Plymouth Mountain Trail

Plymouth Mountain 7,295 ft.

Scenic View Trail

Plymouth Mountain Trail

Homestead Trail

Black Bear Trail

Golden Eagle Trail

Deer Creek

DEER CREEK CANYON PARK

Red Mesa Loop Trail

Phillipsburg

excellent views of Denver and the plains. Climb at a steady rate, and reach a junction with the Scenic View Trail on the left. This is a nice spot to take a break. Go left on the Scenic View Trail as it curves to the north and climbs steadily to the summit of Plymouth Mountain.

There are excellent views to the north and east as you reach the summit at the 2.8-mile mark. Take a short break and enjoy the wonderful views before retracing your route back to the parking area.

Miles and Directions

0.0 Start on the Plymouth Creek Trail.

1.2 Arrive at a junction with the Meadowlark Trail.

1.9 Plymouth Mountain Trail.

2.4 Junction with the Scenic View Trail.

2.8 Reach the summit of Plymouth Mountain. Retrace your steps.

5.6 Arrive back at the trailhead.

48 Reynolds Park Open Space

Tucked away in Kennedy Gulch, this prime piece of open space is about 6 miles south of the town of Conifer. As in other open space areas in Jefferson County, the trails are maintained and marked. A stiff climb to the Eagle's View Trail leads to a spectacular overlook of the South Platte area and panoramic views to the east, west, and south.

Start: From the parking area, go right past the restrooms to the Elkhorn Trail.
Distance: 4.1-mile loop
Hiking time: About 1.5 to 2.5 hours
Difficulty: Moderate
Trail surface: Rocky in sections
Seasons: Year-round

Other trail users: Mountain bikers and equestrians
Canine compatibility: Dogs must be on leash
Maps: Jefferson County Open Space/ Reynolds Park Open Space map
Trail contact: Jefferson County Open Space; (303) 271-5925; http://jeffco.us/open space/index.htm

Finding the trailhead: From Denver, travel west on US 285 to the town of Conifer. Travel through Conifer to Foxton Road. Go left on Foxton Road and drive for 5.2 miles to Reynolds Open Space Park. The parking area is on the right. GPS: N39 28.0056' / W105 14.2127'

The Hike

From the parking area, go right past the restrooms to the Elkhorn Trail. Go right on the Elkhorn Trail and begin a steep climb past several switchbacks toward the Raven's Roost Trail. Yuccas, cacti, and wildflowers grow on this open south-facing slope.

At around the 0.4-mile mark go left on the Raven's Roost Trail and continue climbing into a forest of tall spruce trees up to where the Raven's Roost Trail goes to the left and drops down to a small creek crossing. At around the 1.3-mile mark you arrive at a junction with the Eagle View and Oxen Draw Trails. Go right on the Eagle View Trail and climb steadily through the trees to a ridgeline and a small, open meadow.

Arrive at the overlook, where the Eagle View Trail ends near an old fire pit. Enjoy the spectacular views to the east, south, and west. Looking west you can easily identify the large burn area left by the fire of 1996, which charred more than 12,000 acres of prime Pike National Forest land. Take a few minutes to enjoy the views, then head back down the Eagle View Trail to the Oxen Draw Trail.

Go right on the Oxen Draw Trail and cross the stream several times. Negotiate a few rocky sections, and at the 3.3-mile mark arrive back at the Elkhorn Trail. The Elkhorn Trail is 0.9-mile long and has several interpretive signs that explain local fauna and geology. Feel free to take this side trail to enhance your visit to Reynolds Park. Then follow the Elkhorn Trail for 0.2 mile to the Songbird Trail. Go right on

Reynolds Park Open Space

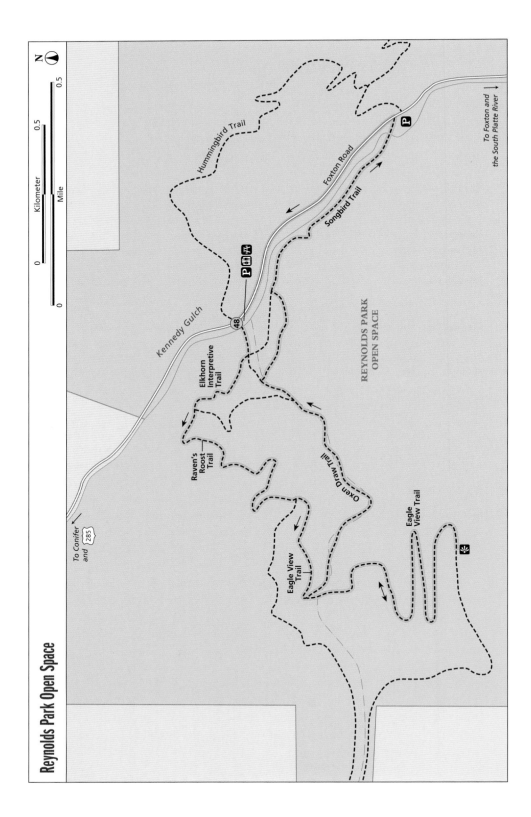

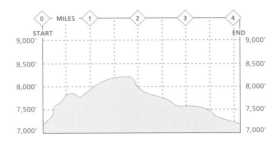

the Songbird Trail and cruise along the stream on a slight downhill grade. Be on the lookout for wildflowers that grow in the late spring and early summer months along the stream.

At the 3.9-mile mark travel over a small wood bridge. Cross the bridge where the trail dumps you at the lower parking area. Go left, up Foxton Road, to the upper parking area, the trailhead, and your car.

Option: At the 4-mile mark cross Foxton Road and take the Hummingbird Trail up the north side of Kennedy Gulch. Loop back to the upper parking, adding 1.3 miles to your hike.

Miles and Directions

0.0   Start by following the Elkhorn Trail toward the Raven's Roost Trail.

0.4   Arrive at a junction with Raven's Roost Trail.

1.3   Arrive at a junction with the Eagle View Trail and Oxen Draw trail. Follow the Eagle View Trail to a great overlook.

2.0   Arrive at a beautiful overlook. Retrace your steps back Oxen Draw Trail.

2.7   Oxen Draw Trail. Go right.

3.3   Arrive at a junction with the Elkhorn Trail.

3.5   Go right on the Songbird Trail.

4.0   Foxton Road.

4.1   Arrive back at the trailhead and parking area.

49 Elk Meadow Park

A rolling, beautiful hike in Elk Meadow Park Wildlife Preserve. On this hike expect to see early season wildflowers, western meadowlarks, prairie grasses, mule deer, ponderosas, tall Douglas firs, and, if you're lucky, bugling elk.

Start: From the parking area, head north on the Sleepy "S" Trail.
Distance: 5.4-mile loop
Hiking time: About 2 to 3 hours
Difficulty: Easy to moderate
Trail surface: Mostly smooth
Seasons: Year-round

Other trail users: Equestrians
Canine compatibility: Dogs not permitted
Maps: Jefferson County Open Space/Elk Meadow Open Space Park map
Trail contact: Jefferson County Open Space; (303) 271-5925; http://jeffco.us/open space/index.htm

Finding the trailhead: From Denver, travel west on I-70 to CO 74 (Evergreen Parkway). Travel 5 miles south on CO 74 to Stagecoach Boulevard. Turn right on Stagecoach Boulevard and travel 1.3 miles to a parking area and trailhead on the right. The hike starts here. GPS: N39 39.4804' / W105 21.2888'

The Hike

From the parking area, head north on the Sleepy "S" Trail. Enjoy level hiking and smooth tread to the junction with the Meadow View Trail. Turn left on the Meadow View Trail and climb through the ponderosas and aspens at a gentle grade to a junction with the Bergen Peak Trail. There are nice views to the north and east to Elk Meadow.

From the trail junction with the Bergen Peak Trail (0.9-mile mark), continue straight on the Meadow View Trail. The trail is fairly smooth and rolls along, with open views of the meadow and to the north and east. Tall grasses grow along with cacti, wildflowers, and pine trees.

At the 1.1-mile mark you reach a junction with the Elkridge Trail and views to the east.

Option: Those of you who want to shorten the hike can make a right on the Elkridge Trail; after a 0.5-mile hike you arrive at a junction with the Sleepy "S"

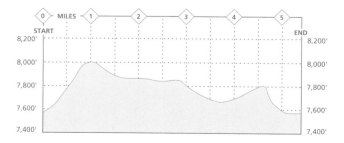

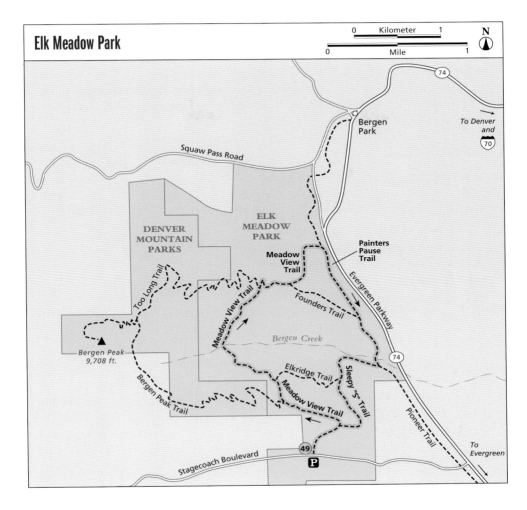

Trail. Go right on the Sleepy "S" Trail and in less than a mile you are back at the parking area.

For this hike, continue on the beautiful, rolling Meadow View Trail heading north, with open views. Be on the lookout for mule deer and other wildlife through this section of the hike. At the 2.1-mile mark you arrive at a junction with the Too Long Trail on the left. This is a nice spot to take a short break. Turn right and continue on the Meadow View Trail, losing elevation and heading to the east and toward CO 74.

After almost 2 miles of beautiful hiking, at the 3-mile mark, you reach a junction with Painters Pause Trail. Go right on the Painters Pause Trail, with CO 74 on your left. Late spring and early summer is a wonderful time to do this hike. The meadow is filled with green prairie grasses, numerous wildflowers, and the beautiful song of the western meadowlark drowning out the sound of the passing cars and trucks on the highway. Look west to the rocky summit of Bergen Peak (9,708 feet).

Roll down the trail and arrive at a junction with the Sleepy "S" Trail at the 4-mile mark. Turn right on the Sleepy "S" Trail and climb past several water bars up into a beautiful meadow. Enjoy beautiful and sometimes steep hiking in a forest of scattered ponderosas. Take a break on a bench just left of the trail. Travel to the first junction with the Meadow View Trail. Turn left on the Meadow View Trail and retrace your steps, dropping back to the trailhead.

Miles and Directions

0.0 Start on the Sleepy "S" Trail, heading north.

0.3 Arrive at a junction with the Meadow View Trail.

0.9 Arrive at a junction with the Bergen Peak Trail.

1.1 Arrive at a junction with the Elkridge Trail.

2.1 Arrive at a junction with the Too Long Trail.

3.0 Arrive at a junction with Painters Pause Trail.

4.0 Arrive at a junction with the Sleepy "S" Trail.

5.4 Arrive back at the trailhead.

50 Bergen Peak

On this beautiful hike up to the summit of Bergen Peak (9,708 feet), you can expect to see wildlife, wildflowers along the trail, and excellent views from on top. This is an excellent hike and a must-do.

Start: From the parking area, head north on the Sleepy "S" Trail.
Distance: 9.2 miles out and back
Hiking time: About 4 to 6 hours
Difficulty: Moderate to strenuous
Trail surface: Steep and rocky; uses several switchbacks to negotiate the steeper sections
Seasons: Mar to Nov

Other trail users: Mountain bikers and equestrians
Canine compatibility: Dogs not permitted
Maps: Jefferson County Open Space/ Elk Meadow Open Space Park map
Trail contact: Jefferson County Open Space; (303) 271-5925; http://jeffco.us/open space/index.htm

Finding the trailhead: From Denver, travel west on I-70 to CO 74 (Evergreen Parkway). Travel 5 miles south on CO 74 to Stagecoach Boulevard. Turn right on Stagecoach Boulevard and travel 1.3 miles to the signed Elk Meadow parking area and trailhead on the right. The hike starts here. GPS: N39 39.4804' / W105 21.2888'

The Hike

From the parking area, head north on the Sleepy "S" Trail. Enjoy level hiking and smooth tread up to a junction with the Meadow View Trail. Turn left on the Meadow View Trail and climb at a gentle grade toward a junction with the Bergen Peak Trail. There are nice views to the north and Elk Meadow. Elk Meadow is an important winter grazing area for elk and mule deer.

Arrive at the Bergen Peak Trail at the 0.9-mile mark. Go left on the Bergen Peak Trail and climb past several steep sections. Water bars and wood steps help to keep erosion in check on the steep part of the trail. Switchback up through the pines, and then reach another steep section with switchbacks. Power up through this section and reach the top of the switchbacks. Take a break and enjoy great views to the north and south.

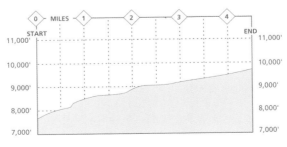

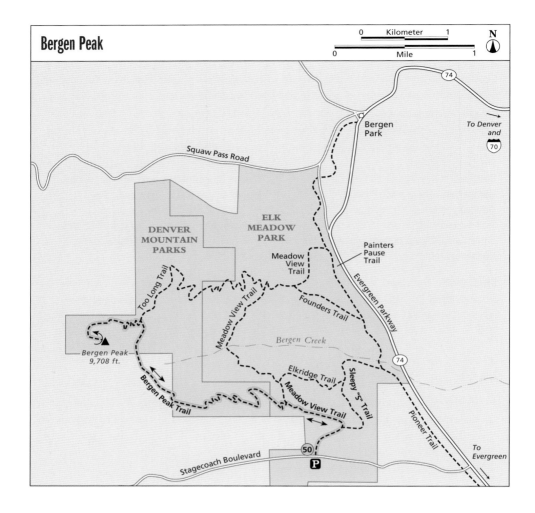

Follow the Bergen Peak Trail as it curves to the north and drops to a junction with Too Long Trail. Hope you enjoyed that downhill; things get steep from here to the summit of the peak.

Turn left, staying on the Bergen Peak Trail. Grind through a steep, rocky section and climb to an overlook with views to the north, east, and south. Take a quick breather and continue to climb three switchbacks. The trail heads to the west and actually drops a short distance before the last climb to the summit. Views to the west and north make the last steep pitch doable.

Follow the steep trail up through a rocky section and reach the summit of Bergen Peak. This is a great spot to relax, eat some lunch, and take in the panoramic views in all directions. Views like this make all that climbing worth it. After taking lots of photographs and a long break, retrace your route back to the trailhead.

This is an extremely popular area with other trail users, and for good reason. Keep in mind that they (mountain bikers and equestrians) have the same rights and privileges that you do. Thank other trail users when they yield to you. To make your hike of Bergen Peak a quiet and more enjoyable experience, do the hike midweek, when there are fewer trail users and a lot more solitude.

Miles and Directions

0.0 Start on the Sleepy "S" Trail.

0.3 Arrive at a junction with the Meadow View Trail.

0.9 Arrive at a junction with the Bergen Peak Trail.

3.6 Arrive at a junction with the Too Long Trail.

4.6 Arrive at the summit of Bergen Peak. Retrace your steps.

9.2 Arrive back at the trailhead.

51 Chief Mountain

Though this is a short hike up to the rocky summit of Chief Mountain (11,709 feet), the trail gains over 1,100 feet in 1.5 miles. But once on top of Chief Mountain you are rewarded for all that hard work with spectacular views to the north and south, and eastward to the plains.

Start: From the pullout, cross Squaw Pass Road and access the unmarked trail leading into the trees.
Distance: 3.0 miles out and back
Hiking time: About 1.5 to 2 hours
Difficulty: Moderate
Trail surface: Fairly smooth on the lower section; quite rocky near the summit

Seasons: Spring to fall
Other trail users: None
Canine compatibility: Dogs must be on leash
Maps: Illustrated Idaho Springs/ Georgetown/ Loveland Pass #104
Trail contact: Arapaho National Forest; (970) 295-6600

Finding the trailhead: From Denver, take I-70 west to exit 252 (CO 74/Evergreen Parkway). Follow Evergreen Parkway (CO 74) south for just over 2.9 miles to CO 103/Squaw Pass Road. Go right on CO 103, and drive for 12.1 miles to a pullout on the right side of the road. The hike starts here. GPS: N39 40.5660' / W105 31.1020'

The Hike

From the pullout, cross Squaw Pass Road and pick up a trail that switchbacks up a steep hill. Pass a cement post marked 290, and climb into the tall spruce trees. Pass a small kiosk. Arrive at Old Squaw Pass Road at around the 0.2-mile mark. Cross the road to the Chief Mountain Trail. The sign says 2 miles to the summit, but by my GPS system, it is really only 1.3 miles.

Climb to a saddle, with Papoose Mountain (11,174 feet) on the left and Chief Mountain looming high above you on the right. The trail now makes a steady climb through the trees on the north side of Chief Mountain, making use of long switchbacks, and quickly gains altitude. At around the 0.9-mile mark the trail breaks out of the trees and enters alpine tundra. Dramatic views open to the west to Mount Evans, north to the Indian Peaks and Longs Peak, and east to the plains.

The trail cuts through the open tundra and heads west, passing two switchbacks. Lichen-covered rocks are scattered everywhere, and small alpine flowers grow in

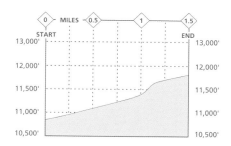

Chief Mountain

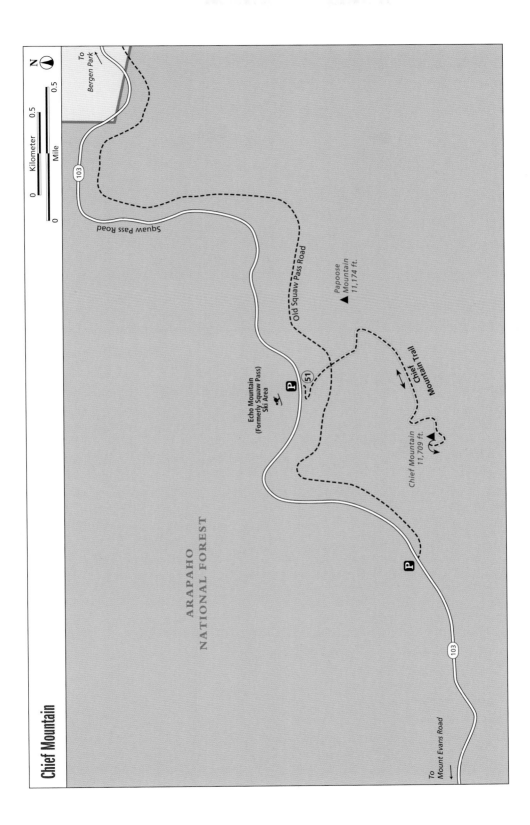

Spectacular views from the summit of Chief Mountain

the rocky soil. The views are spectacular and the hiking is wonderful through this section of the trail.

Reach a huge, flattop boulder along the side of the trail. Stop here and take in the views. Soon gain the summit saddle, and travel through a sparse forest of stunted bristlecone pines and subalpine firs. Panoramic views and colorful rocks surround you as you quickly gain the rock-covered summit. Enjoy the views, take a break, and don't rush to leave this spot. Longs Peak and Mount Meeker are far to the north, Mount Evans and Mount Bierstadt are to the west, Pikes Peak is to the south, and Denver and the plains are to the east. It's hard to believe that you can have these views on an 11,709-foot summit.

Retrace your route back to the trailhead. Once back at your car look down and to the north to the new Echo Mountain ski park.

Miles and Directions

0.0 Start by crossing Squaw Pass Road and climbing past a post marked 290.

0.2 Reach Old Squaw Pass Road.

0.3 Papoose Mountain is on the left.

0.9 Reach open alpine tundra.

1.2 Arrive at the summit saddle.

1.5 Arrive at the summit of Chief Mountain.

3.0 Arrive back at the trailhead.

52 Mount Bierstadt

Everybody wants to do a "fourteener," and this is one of the most accessible near the Front Range. The trail is well marked and easy to the follow, with little chance of getting off track. The views of the surrounding peaks are spectacular and become more impressive the higher you climb.

Start: From the parking area, head east to access the signed Mount Bierstadt trail.
Distance: 7.4 miles out and back
Hiking time: About 4 to 6 hours
Difficulty: Moderate to strenuous
Trail surface: Well maintained, extremely smooth for first 2.5 miles; upper section is rocky and steep
Seasons: June to Oct

Other trail users: None
Canine compatibility: Dogs must be on leash
Maps: Trails Illustrated Idaho Springs/ Georgetown/Loveland Pass #104
Trail contact: South Platte Ranger District/ USDA Forest Service; (303) 275-5610
Other: Camping is available at the Guanella Pass Campground, located 2 miles east of the trailhead.

Finding the trailhead: From Denver, follow I-70 west to Georgetown. Travel through Georgetown to Guanella Pass Road. Follow Guanella Pass Road for 10 miles to the Mount Bierstadt Trailhead on the left. The hike starts here. GPS: N39 35.4799' / W105 42.3695'

The Hike

From the trailhead, the Mount Bierstadt Trail drops into the willows toward Deadmans Lake on the left. The route then travels through heavy willows and wet areas on several new wood bridges. Before the bridges were established in this area, the trail was hard to follow and extremely wet. Thanks to the forest service and all the volunteers who helped construct the bridges and worked on the trail. There are several tarns in this area, and wildflowers grow profusely in the moist soil.

After a mile of easy hiking, you cross Scott Gomer Creek. This can be dangerous during early summer runoff, so use caution during times of high runoff. After the stream crossing, the trail begins to climb through the willows on smooth tread; this is enjoyable hiking.

At about the 1.5-mile mark, the trail climbs steeply to a large, open meadow. Mount Bierstadt (14,060 feet) dominates the skyline in the east, with the rocky, jagged summit of The Sawtooth to the left. The steep, rocky walls of The Sawtooth face to the northwest and appear

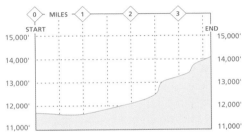

Spectacular alpine hiking

dark and ominous for most of the day, creating an impressive and intimidating alpine cirque.

The meadow you travel through is home to the rare Uncompahgre butterfly. This small insect makes its home in the snow willows that grow on tundra in high alpine meadows. Be careful not to go off the trail as the tundra flowers, grasses, and willows are extremely fragile and susceptible to human and animal intrusion.

Things get a little more serious from this point on. The trail becomes rockier, with sections of stone steps making the going easier as you climb up to a shelf running south. The lay of the land changes drastically as you gain altitude and shoot back to the north into a large boulder field below the south saddle of Mount Bierstadt. Rock cairns mark the way up through the boulder field and keep you going in the right direction.

For some strange reason the summit of Mount Bierstadt, off and up to the left, looks closer than it really is. Don't get discouraged: Keep cranking and before you know it you arrive in a somewhat level boulder field along the south saddle. This is a good spot to take a break and enjoy the panoramic views. Ramble over to the saddle and peer down at Frozen Lake, neatly tucked below. If the weather is changing for the worse, this is not the place to be. Summer thunderstorms are extremely dangerous, and exposed ridges are not the places to be hanging out.

The trail now goes north along the south ridgeline of Mount Bierstadt and into the boulders. Small cairns mark the way along this strenuous section to the summit.

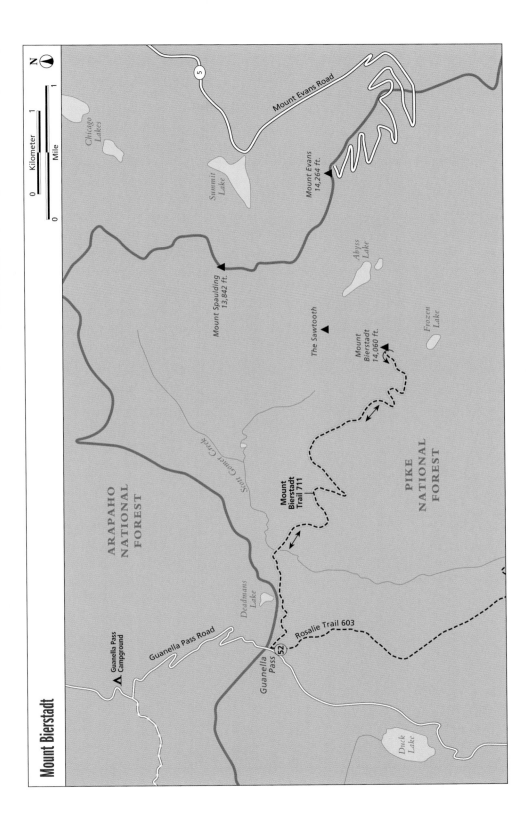

Mount Bierstadt

N

Kilometer
0   1

Mile
0   1

Guanella Pass Campground

Guanella Pass Road

ARAPAHO NATIONAL FOREST

Deadmans Lake

Guanella Pass

52

Rosalie Trail 603

Scott Gomer Creek

Mount Bierstadt Trail 711

The Sawtooth

Mount Bierstadt 14,060 ft.

PIKE NATIONAL FOREST

Frozen Lake

Abyss Lake

Mount Spaulding 13,842 ft.

Summit Lake

Chicago Lakes

Mount Evans 14,264 ft.

Mount Evans Road

5

Duck Lake

After less than 0.25 mile of steep hiking, arrive at the summit of Mount Bierstadt and take a well-deserved rest. Looking to the north you can see the summit of Mount Evans (14,264 feet), Abyss Lake, and the paved Mount Evans Road. Turn to the west and the twin fourteeners, Grays (14,270 feet) and Torreys (14,267 feet) Peaks, stand high in the western sky. The views are panoramic, spectacular, and extend in all directions. This is why you climb a fourteener.

After your rest, turn around and retrace your route back to the trailhead.

Miles and Directions

0.0 Start from the parking area and follow the signed Mount Bierstadt Trail 711 into the willows.

0.2 The trail passes Deadmans Lake on the left.

1.0 Cross a small creek.

1.5 Begin a steep climb.

3.3 Arrive at the South saddle and wonderfuls views.

3.7 Arrive at the summit and enjoy panoramic views. Retrace your steps.

7.4 Arrive back at the trailhead.

53 Grays and Torreys Peaks

A great outing leads up to the twin summits of Grays and Torreys Peaks. This strenuous hike reaches the summit of Grays Peak in 4-plus miles, with 3,500 feet of elevation gain, and there is an option to climb Torreys Peak just to the west. Spectacular views, beautiful alpine peaks, and colorful summer wildflowers are what you can expect on this impressive alpine outing.

Start: From the parking area, cross Stevens Gulch Road and then over a small footbridge to the signed Grays Peak trail 54.
Distance: 8.4 miles out and back to the summit of Grays Peak
Hiking time: About 4 to 7 hours
Difficulty: Moderate to strenuous
Trail surface: The lower section is fairly smooth and well maintained. The upper section is steep, narrow, and rocky. Much work has been done on the upper section of the trail, so stay on the path and restrain from cutting switchbacks.
Seasons: June to Oct
Other trail users: None
Canine compatibility: Dogs must be on leash
Maps: Trails Illustrated Idaho Springs/ Georgetown/Loveland Pass #104

Trail contact: Clear Creek Ranger District/ USDA Forest Service; (970) 295-6600; www .fs.usda.gov/contactus/arp/about-forest/ contactus
Special considerations: These two peaks are considered to be easy fourteeners. Don't be fooled; they should demand your respect. Be prepared for rapid weather changes, lightning, hail, rain, or snow any time of the year. Bring a wind jacket or raincoat, and extra clothing. Bring food and two quarts of water. The peaks see heavy hiker traffic during weekends in the summer months. Plan your trip during the week for a more enjoyable and peaceful experience. Plan an early start during the months of July and August to avoid thunderstorms, which can be extremely violent and scary. Plan on being off the summit by noon during these months.

Finding the trailhead: From Denver, follow I-70 west to Georgetown. Continue 6 miles past Georgetown on I-70 and exit the interstate at Bakerville. Cross over the interstate and follow Stevens Gulch Road for 3 miles south to the trailhead and parking. GPS: N39 39.3957' / W105 47.0459'

The Hike

From the trailhead, cross Stevens Gulch Road and travel over a bridge to the start of the Grays Peak Trail 54. Past the bridge the trail climbs at a modest grade up through dense willows on both sides of the trail. The trail hugs the eastern flank of Kelso Mountain (13,164 feet), with spectacular views south to Mount Edwards and Grays and Torreys Peaks. Looking east, at the base of McClellan Mountain, you can see the remnants of the old Stevens Mine. The old decaying buildings and piles of tailings are all that remain of what was once the site of a large mining operation.

At around the 2-mile mark, reach a kiosk with trail information. This is a great place to take a short break before tackling the steep, strenuous hike ahead. Beyond

The author and Nala on the summit

the kiosk, climb through an often wet section of trail into a large cirque below the impressive summits of Grays and Torreys Peaks. The trail cuts back to the east through a very rocky section, and gains altitude very quickly. The hiking becomes laborious as you break out into open tundra, following long switchbacks below the north face of Grays Peak. Beautiful views open to Torreys Peak to the west, and back down valley to Kelso and McClellan Mountains.

At around the 3.5-mile mark reach a trail junction and marker. The upper trail to the summit of Grays Peak used to be an old horse trail that carried tourists to the top of the mountain. The Colorado Fourteener Initiative made a number of improvements to the trail in the summer of 2001, and established logical trails to both summits. Going right will take you to a saddle between Grays and Torreys Peaks. Go left, following the switchbacks that steeply lead to the summit of Grays Peak.

Reach the summit at around the 4.2-mile mark and enjoy spectacular views in all directions. This is why you climb a fourteener. You feel like you are standing on top of the world. Take a short break before retracing your route back to the trailhead.

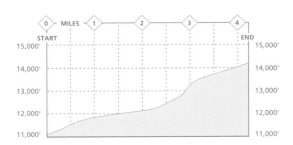

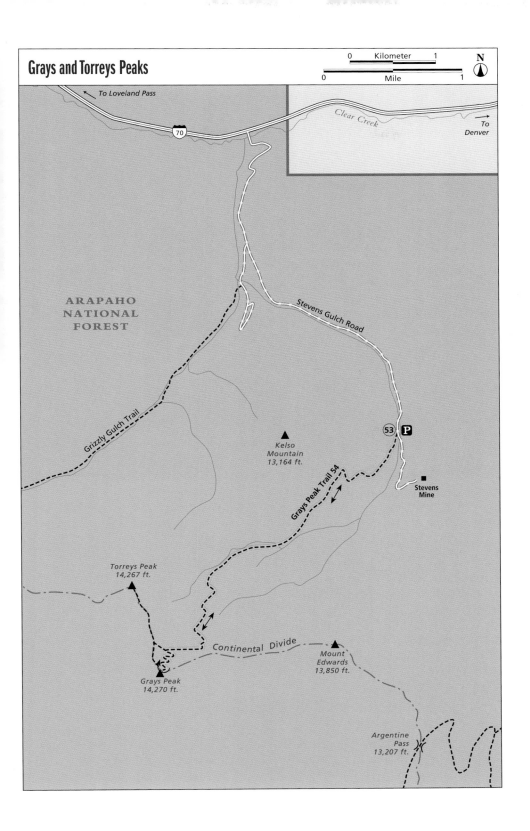

Grays and Torreys Peaks

0   Kilometer   1

0   Mile   1

N

To Loveland Pass

Clear Creek

To Denver

70

ARAPAHO
NATIONAL
FOREST

Stevens Gulch Road

Grizzly Gulch Trail

Kelso
Mountain
13,164 ft.

53 P

Grays Peak Trail 54

Stevens
Mine

Torreys Peak
14,267 ft.

Continental Divide

Mount
Edwards
13,850 ft.

Grays Peak
14,270 ft.

Argentine
Pass
13,207 ft.

Mother and young mountain goats

Option: From the summit of Grays Peak, follow the obvious ridgeline to the north. Reach a saddle between Grays and Torreys Peaks, with a trail on the right. Continue up the ridge, quickly gaining the summit of Torreys Peak (14,267 feet) and your second fourteener in a day. Retrace your route back to the saddle and follow the trail back to the trailhead.

Miles and Directions

0.0   Start by crossing Stevens Gulch Road and the bridge to the start of Grays Peak Trail 54.

2.0   Arrive at a kiosk.

3.5   Arrive at a trail junction. Continue straight.

4.2   Reach the summit of Grays Peak. Retrace your steps.

8.4   Arrive back at the trailhead.

South of Denver and Colorado Springs Area

54 Columbine Open Space

This open space parcel just south of Castle Rock offers two short trails just above Plum Creek and I-25. Columbine Open Space provides a buffer from ever-encroaching growth along the I-25 corridor.

Start: From the parking area, pass the kiosk and travel south on the South Loop Trail.
Distance: 2.6 miles for both loops
Hiking time: About 1 to 2 hours
Difficulty: Easy
Trail surface: Smooth
Seasons: Year-round

Other trail users: Mountain bikers and equestrians
Canine compatibility: Dogs not permitted
Maps: Douglas County/Columbine Open Space map
Trail contact: Douglas County Open Space; (303) 660-7495; www.douglas.co.us/open space

Finding the trailhead: From Castle Rock, travel south on I-25 to exit 174 (Tomah Road). Travel over the interstate and north (left) on the Frontage Road to the entrance of Columbine Open Space. Follow the sign to the parking area and trailhead, which is near a large red barn. GPS: N39 16.5517' / W104 55.3825'

The Hike

This is a great little hike to get the young ones outdoors, so bring the kids along. From the parking area, pass the kiosk and travel south on the South Loop Trail. Pass a bench and drop down a short hill to the start of the first loop. Go right and follow the South Loop Trail through an open area, with Plum Creek on the right, filled with willows and cottonwoods. The trail makes a sharp left and heads back north, with railroad tracks on your right. There are nice views to the north and west to Devils Head.

Make a short climb back to the parking area at 1.3 miles and the start of the north loop. Pass the kiosk and follow the wide path across the road and down into an open area, with nice-looking cottonwoods and Plum Creek on the left. The trail makes a short climb and reaches a level area and bench. Go right and follow the start of the North Loop Trail with railroad tracks on the right. Private property surrounds the

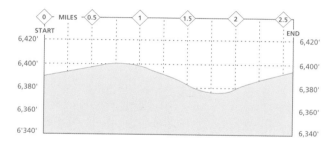

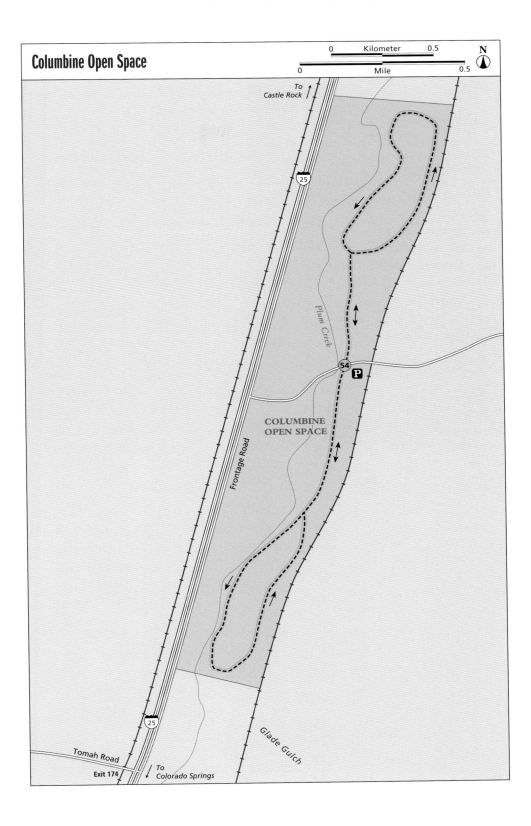

trail, and the ever-expanding sprawl can be seen to the north. There are excellent views to the east and west.

The trail curves to the south and heads back to the trailhead. Retrace your route from the bench and hike back to the trailhead and parking area.

Be aware of the rattlesnake signs along the trail. Rattlesnakes like to sun themselves on the trail during the summer months.

Miles and Directions

0.0   Start from the parking area and follow the South Loop Trail.

0.2   Arrive at a bench.

0.3   Start of the South Loop Trail.

0.9   End of the South loop.

1.3   Back at the trailhead and start of the north loop.

1.7   Start of the North Loop Trail.

1.9   Arrive at a bench.

2.2   End of the North loop. Retrace your steps.

2.6   Arrive back at the trailhead.

55 Palmer Park

This fantastic hike through a city park has excellent views of Pikes Peak and the Garden of the Gods. Bizarre rock formations, wildflowers, and fields filled with blooming yuccas all contribute to an excellent hike within the city limits of Colorado Springs. There are many trails that crisscross Palmer Park. Follow the map and mileage cues, and you shouldn't have any problems enjoying this beautiful area.

Start: From the parking area, access the Greencrest Trail by going past the northernmost baseball field and heading toward power lines at an old service road directly beyond centerfield.
Distance: 5.7-mile loop
Hiking time: About 2 to 3.5 hours
Difficulty: Moderate
Trail surface: Varies from very smooth to extremely rocky

Seasons: Year-round
Other trail users: Mountain bikers and equestrians
Canine compatibility: Dogs must be on leash
Maps: City of Colorado Springs Parks and Recreation/Palmer Park map
Trail contact: City of Colorado Springs; (719) 385-5940; www.springsgov.com /sectionindex.aspx?sectionid=17

Finding the trailhead: Travel south on I-25 from Denver, past the Air Force Academy to Academy Boulevard. Follow Academy Boulevard south to Maizeland Road. Turn right onto Maizeland Road and make a quick right into Palmer Park. Turn right into a large parking area near the ballparks. The hike starts here. GPS: N38 52.1969' / W104 45.4965'

The Hike

From the parking area, access the Greencrest Trail by going past the northernmost baseball field and heading toward power lines at an old service road directly beyond centerfield. The Greencrest Trail is well marked and follows the power lines on a wide dirt trail just east of the dog park. Follow the Greencrest Trail past two private driveways and up through two picnic areas.

At around the 0.6-mile mark reach a trail junction. Follow the Greencrest Trail up and right on a very rocky trail. The Greencrest Trail winds up past several rock formations and gains a ridge. Follow the signs for the Greencrest Trail and drop into

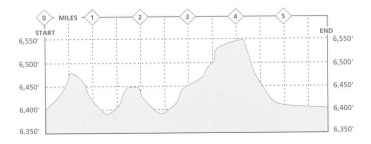

Rocky Mountain Columbine, Colorado's state flower

an open meadow under the power lines. This is nice hiking through a meadow filled with tall prairie grasses, yuccas, and scattered ponderosas

The trail leads you past a Boy Scout camp on the left, and brings you to a road at the 1.5-mile mark. Cross the road and reach the Palmer Crest Trail. Go right on the Palmer Crest Trail, on very narrow tread under the power lines. The trail climbs up a short hill and then winds down to a large parking area. Go left, up past the restrooms and around the volleyball court, to a junction with the Templeton Trail.

Go right on the Templeton Trail, through thick stands of Gambel oak, to a trail junction. Go right, following the Templeton Trail and heading north. The trail climbs through a very rocky section and reaches a high point with a strange rock formation on the right. Drop a short distance and then climb again on rocky tread, reaching an overlook. There are great views west to Pikes Peak and the red-colored cliffs of the Garden of the Gods.

Past the overlook, the trail drops down and cuts under the base of a large sandstone cliff. Beautiful hiking through this section leads you to a trail junction at the 3-mile mark. Go left and up on extremely rocky tread, hugging the base of large sandstone bluffs.

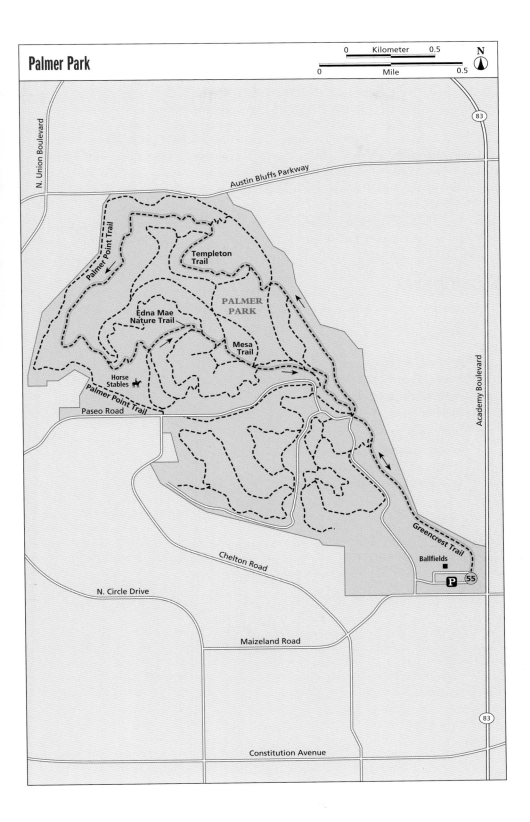

Enjoy excellent views to the west as you climb up to a trail junction at the 3.4-mile mark. Go right and down on the North Canon Trail, and drop past several rock switchbacks to a parking area, horse stable, and the Edna Mae Nature Trail. Go left, past the large trail sign, onto the Edna Mae Nature Trail, which leads into a narrow gulch.

Climb several rocky steps to a trail junction at the 3.9-mile mark. Go right at the trail marker, heading up to the Mesa Trail and a large open mesa filled with yuccas. Head toward the east side of the mesa, to a gate, road, and parking area. Access the trail across the road, going left at the trail marker on the Palmer Point Trail.

The Palmer Point Trail parallels the road on nice smooth tread. At the 4.5-mile mark, the trail crosses the road and then goes right through the ponderosas to its junction with the Greencrest Trail. Follow the Greencrest Trail back to the parking area and the end of the hike.

Miles and Directions

0.0 Start from the parking and veer northeast to the start of the Greencrest Trail.

0.6 Arrive at a trail junction; go right following the Greencrest Trail.

1.5 Road.

1.8 Arrive at parking area.

1.9 Arrive at a junction with Templeton Trail. Go right on the Templeton Trail.

2.5 Arrive at a nice overlook.

3.0 Trail junction. Go left.

3.4 Junction with the North Canon Trail.

3.7 Junction with the Edna Mae Nature Trail.

3.9 Junction with Mesa Trail.

4.1 Arrive at the well-named Yucca Mesa.

4.2 Junction with Palmer Point Trail.

4.5 Cross a service road.

4.7 Back at the Greencrest Trail.

5.7 Arrive back at the trailhead.

56 Barr Trail

This great hike heads up the lower section of the world-famous Barr Trail, which reaches the summit of Pikes Peak (14,115 feet), the highest mountain in the Colorado Springs area. This hike climbs the steep switchbacks on the lower section of the trail, and ends at a stunning overlook on the Eagle's Nest Trail.

Start: From the parking area, access the well-marked Barr Trail just behind the kiosk.
Distance: 6.4 miles out and back
Hiking time: About 2.5 to 4 hours
Difficulty: Strenuous
Trail surface: Steep and rocky in sections
Seasons: Year-round; can be snow-packed in the winter months
Other trail users: Mountain bikers and equestrians

Canine compatibility: Dogs must be on leash
Maps: Trails Illustrated Pikes Peak/Canon City #137
Trail contact: Pikes Peak National Forest; (719) 636-1602; www.gorp.com /parks-guide/travel-ta-pike-national-forest-hiking-colorado-sidwcmdev_066073.html #ixzz1jw1diSgJ

Finding the trailhead: From the junction of I-25 and US 24 in Colorado Springs, travel 5.4 miles west on US 24 to the first Manitou Springs exit. Go right on Manitou Avenue and travel 1.4 mile to Ruxton Avenue. Go left on Ruxton Avenue, passing the Cog Railroad on the left, to Hydro Street. Make a right on Hydro Street; it dead-ends at the trailhead parking lot. GPS: N38 51.1871' / W104 56.0200'

The Hike

This section of the Barr Trail used to be one of my favorite training runs back in the early '80s, when I was living in the Colorado Springs area. The section described here tackles the lower Barr Trail, climbing the famous switchbacks that cut a narrow path up the steep flank of Rocky Mountain.

From the parking area, access the well-marked Barr Trail and begin what seems like an endless climb up steep switchbacks toward Englemann Canyon. Pass a junction with a trail that shoots left, down to Ruxton Creek. At the 1-mile mark, pass a marked sign noting you are at 7,200 feet. Several large granite boulders grace the steep hillsides, and at the 1.8-mile mark the boulders offer great views of Englemann Canyon and a great place to take a well-deserved break.

The trail continues to switchback up the steep grade, and then passes through a rock tunnel around the 2.4-mile mark. Enjoy the relief from the steep climbing. At the 2.6-mile mark, you reach a junction with Incline Trail. Take the Incline Trail, and then bear left on a spur trail that leads to a junction with the Eagle's Nest Trail at the 3-mile mark.

The lower section of this gorgeous trail

Follow the Eagle's Nest Trail, dropping down to an overlook with amazing views of the city of Colorado Springs and the plains beyond. After a nice rest, retrace your route back to the parking area.

Bring ample water and some energy food. The trail is steep and strenuous for being so short a hike.

Barr Trail

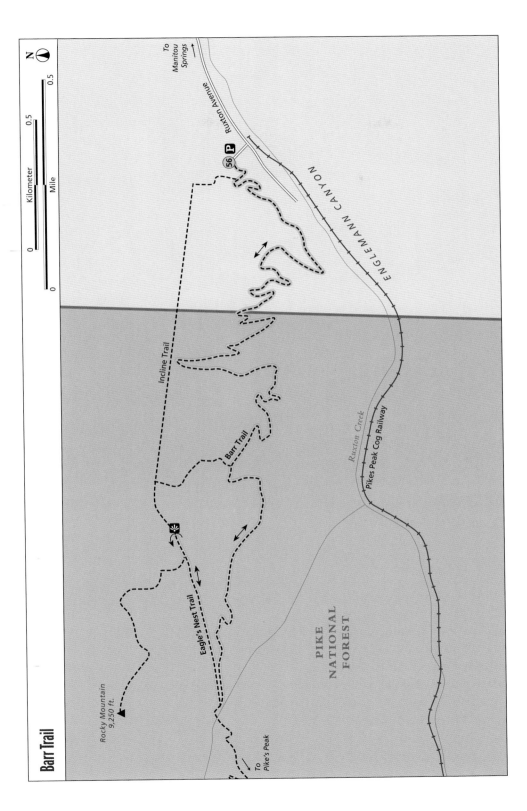

Rocky Mountain
9,250 ft.

To
Pike's Peak

Eagle's Nest Trail

Incline Trail

Barr Trail

PIKE
NATIONAL
FOREST

Ruxton Creek

Pikes Peak Cog Railway

ENGLEMANN CANYON

Ruxton Avenue

To
Manitou
Springs

P
56

N

Kilometer
0   0.5   0.5

Mile
0   0.5

An old Cog Railway engine

Miles and Directions

0.0   Access the trailhead near the kiosk at the parking area.

1.0   Arrive at the 7,200-foot marker.

1.8   Arrive at the overlook; take a nice break and enjoy the views.

2.4   Pass through a rock tunnel.

2.6   Arrive at the Incline Trail junction.

3.0   Junction of the Eagle's Nest Trail.

3.2   Arrive at the overlook and some picnic tables.

6.4   Arrive back at the trailhead.

57 Section 16/Palmer Trail

This beautiful and popular hike leads through the foothills west of Colorado Springs. An old-growth pine forest, cool mountain streams, and spectacular vistas are the main attractions on this hike. You can hike this loop counterclockwise, but the description goes in a clockwise direction. Enjoy: This is one of the best hikes near Colorado Springs.

Start: From the parking area, walk west on Lower Gold Camp Road to High Drive.
Distance: 5.8-mile loop
Hiking time: About 2 to 3 hours
Difficulty: Moderate
Trail surface: Mostly smooth; rocky for last 2 miles, heading back to trailhead
Seasons: Year-round; can be snowy in the winter months on the north-facing sections of the trail
Other trail users: Mountain bikers and equestrians

Canine compatibility: Dogs must be on leash
Maps: Trails Illustrated Pikes Peak/Canon City #137
Trail contact: Pikes Peak Ranger District; (719) 636-1602; www.gorp.com/parks-guide/travel-ta-pike-national-forest-hiking-colorado-sidwcmdev_066073 .html#ixzz1jw1diSgJ. Parks, Recreation & Cultural Services; (719) 385-5940; www.springsgov.com/sectionindex.aspx?sectionid=17

Finding the trailhead: From Colorado Springs, travel west on US 24 to 26th Street. Turn left on 26th Street and go to a four-way stop at Lower Gold Camp Road. Turn right onto Lower Gold Camp Road and travel 1.5 miles to the Section 16 Trailhead parking area on the right. GPS: N38 49.2247' / W104 53.2484'

The Hike

When I lived in Colorado Springs, this was one of my favorite trail runs. I have run this trail at least a hundred times, and must say I enjoyed every one of those forays into the Hunter's Run drainage. The views are spectacular, wildflowers and yuccas bloom in the summer months, and the old-growth pines are beautiful.

From the parking area, follow Lower Gold Camp Road west to High Drive. At the stop sign, continue straight through a gate and follow High Drive, with Bear Creek on the right. The road (and you) climb at a steady rate past several rock formations on the steep hillsides. Bear Creek switches to the left at around the 0.6-mile mark. At around the 0.9-mile mark, look to the right for a trail coming straight out of a fence line. Ignore this trail and go a short distance up the road to the Palmer Trailhead at around the 1-mile mark.

Turn right at an old metal gate onto the Palmer Trail and head into a small open meadow. Follow the trail up to a junction at the 1.2-mile mark. Straight ahead lie the ruins of an old Boy Scout camp. Go right, up a switchback and into the trees. The

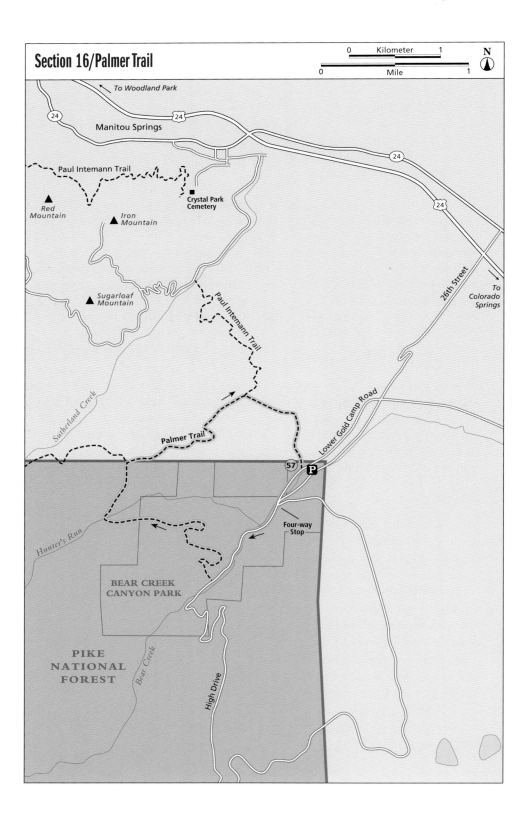

Section 16/Palmer Trail

0 Kilometer 1

0 Mile 1

N

To Woodland Park

24

24

Manitou Springs

24

Paul Intemann Trail

Crystal Park Cemetery

Red Mountain

Iron Mountain

Sugarloaf Mountain

Paul Intemann Trail

26th Street

To Colorado Springs

Sutherland Creek

Lower Gold Camp Road

Palmer Trail

57

P

Hunter's Run

Four-way Stop

BEAR CREEK CANYON PARK

PIKE NATIONAL FOREST

Bear Creek

High Drive

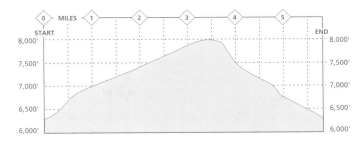

trail climbs steeply at first, then recedes to a nice grade through the dense forest. The hiking is pretty straightforward, with the Hunter's Run drainage appearing down to the right. Occasional views through the pines to the east and south add to the overall beauty of the hike.

The trail switches to the west side of the hill and then climbs past a rocky section, with views of the rocky Tenney Crags and Mount Arthur. The trail comes back to the east on a very narrow section, and then meets beautiful Hunter's Run at the 2.7-mile mark. Do yourself a favor and take a short break at this beautiful mountain stream.

Past the stream, the trail cuts a narrow line across the steep hill and heads north up to a trail junction. There are great views south and east to Colorado Springs. From the junction, go right on Palmer Trail up to the high point of the hike. Enjoy the views across an open area, then dive back into the trees and arrive at a trail junction at the 4-mile mark. Go left and drop down the steep switchback to a section of very rocky and loose tread.

The trail becomes quite steep and soon drops you into a small, open area with several spur trails. Go right, following the Palmer Trail down through a rocky section to a junction with the Paul Intemann Nature Trail and level ground. At the Paul Intemann Nature Trail go right on the Palmer Trail through the Gambel oak, with great views to a series of hogback ridges. The trail now has open views to the north of the Garden of the Gods. Travel down a series of steep switchbacks, where the trail ends abruptly at the parking area.

Miles and Directions

0.0 Start by following Lower Gold Camp Road west to High Drive.

0.3 High Drive.

0.9 Pass a trail junction on the right.

1.0 Go right at the Palmer Trailhead.

1.2 A spur trail leads to old ruins.

2.7 Cross Hunter's Run.

3.3 Arrive at an unmarked trail junction.

4.0 Go left down a steep rocky section.

4.9 Arrive at a junction with Paul Intemann Trail.

5.8 Arrive back at the trailhead.

58 Mount Cutler Trail

This short, beautiful trail with amazing views to the south and west makes for a great family hike, with a gradual climb leading to a stunning overlook.

Start: From the parking area, access the signed Mount Cutler Trail just beyond the kiosk.
Distance: 2.4 miles out and back
Hiking time: About 1 to 2 hours
Difficulty: Moderate
Trail surface: Rocky in sections, with steep drop-offs
Seasons: Year-round; can be snow-packed in the winter months

Other trail users: Equestrians
Canine compatibility: Dogs must be on leash
Maps: City of Colorado Springs Parks and Recreation trail map for North Cheyenne Canyon
Trail contact: City of Colorado Springs Parks and Recreation; (719) 385-5940; www.springsgov.com/sectionindex.aspx?sectionid

Finding the trailhead: From the intersection of I-25 and US 24 in Colorado Springs, go west on US 24 to 21st Street. Go south (left) on 21st Street, which changes into Cresta Road. Follow Cresta Road to Cheyenne Boulevard. Go right on Cheyenne Boulevard to a fork in the road. Take the right fork, which is North Cheyenne Canyon Road. Follow the road for 1.5 miles to the trailhead on the left. GPS: N38 47.2451' /W104 52.4337'

The Hike

This is a straightforward hike that takes you to an overlook with spectacular views to the south, east, and west. The Mount Cutler Trail has a gentle grade as you climb from the trailhead. The trail levels out below a huge red rock, and then climbs to a saddle at 0.7 mile. Enjoy great views looking east and west.

From the saddle, the trail bears left and traverses across an exposed slope with views to Seven Falls. The closer you get to the summit, the more open and spectacular the views become. Reach the summit and enjoy panoramic views in all directions.

Retrace your route back to the trailhead.

Miles and Directions

0.0   Begin the gentle ascent up the nicely maintained trail to the overlook.
0.7   Arrive at the saddle.
1.2   Reach the overlook, take a nice break, and enjoy the views.
2.4   Arrive back at the trailhead.

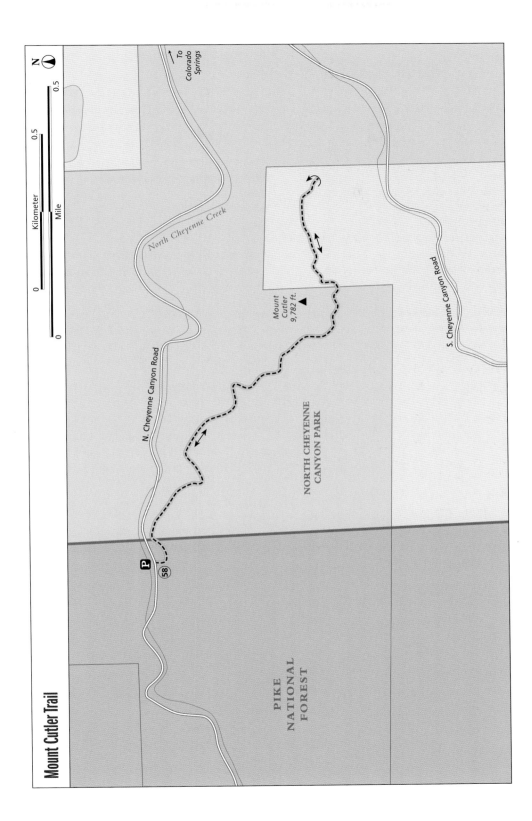

Mount Cutler Trail

N. Cheyenne Canyon Road

North Cheyenne Creek

To Colorado Springs

Mount Cutler 9,782 ft.

NORTH CHEYENNE CANYON PARK

S. Cheyenne Canyon Road

PIKE NATIONAL FOREST

P

58

Kilometer

Mile

0   0.5   0.5

N

59 Paul Intemann Nature Trail

A great hike starts just off Ruxton Avenue in downtown Manitou Springs. Beautiful views of Pikes Peak, Williams Canyon, and the Garden of the Gods Park can be seen from this year-round trail, which sees a fair amount of foot and bike travel.

Start: From the parking area, access the start of the Paul Intemann Nature Trail at the east end of the parking area.
Distance: 5.4 miles out and back
Hiking time: About 1.5 to 2.5 hours
Difficulty: Moderate
Trail surface: Lots of Pikes Peak pea gravel
Seasons: Year-round

Other trail users: Mountain bikers and equestrians
Canine compatibility: Dogs must be on leash
Maps: Trails Illustrated Pikes Peak/Canon City #137
Trail contact: Trails and Open Space Coalition (formerly Pikes Peak Area Trails Coalition); (719) 633-6884

Finding the trailhead: From the junction of I-25 and US 24 in Colorado Springs, travel west on US 24 to Manitou Springs. Travel through Manitou Springs to Ruxton Avenue. Go left on Ruxton Avenue for 1.5 miles to the trailhead on the left. GPS: N38 51. 2400' / W104 55.3725'

The Hike

From the parking area, access the start of the Paul Intemann Nature Trail and head into the trees along a small creek. The trail crosses a small footbridge and quickly reaches an old service road. Go right on the road and climb to two metal posts with a chain going across. There is a sign marking the Paul Intemann Nature Trail by the left post.

Go around the chain and climb steeply up the loose gravel road. The trail is well marked and quickly turns east at a drainage on the right. Follow the old road, lined with yuccas and Gambel oak, up to a bench on the left at an overlook. Enjoy views to the east and west, and north to the Garden of the Gods.

The trail climbs to a junction with the Red Mountain Trail on the right. Remain on the Intemann trail past the junction. The trail drops down a series of steep steps to

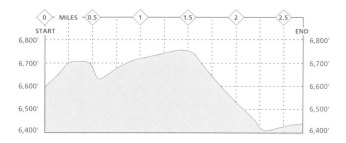

Paul Intemann Nature Trail

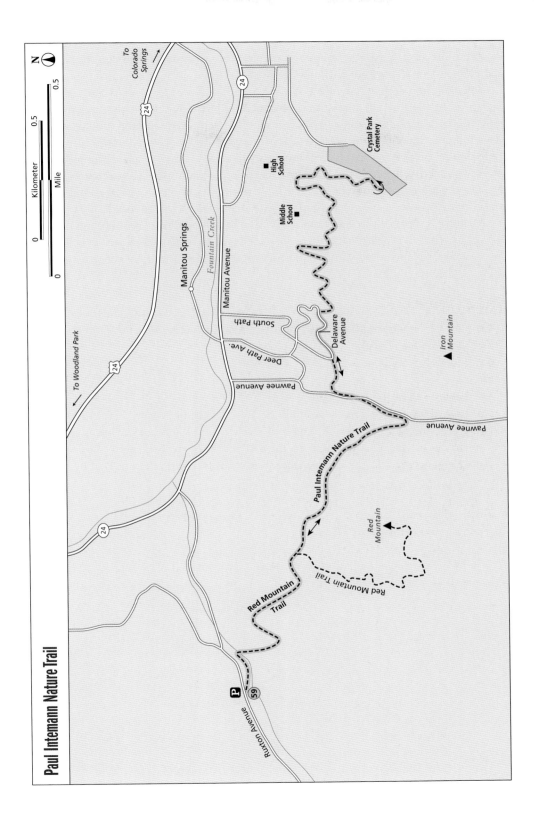

a wood footbridge. Cross the bridge and drop quickly to a road. Go left on the road, and at the 1.4-mile mark go right past some pillars down into a small gulch.

The trail then dumps you onto Delaware Avenue. Follow Delaware Avenue, making a right at the 1.7-mile mark past a small playground. Follow the tight singletrack trail through stands of pinyon and juniper trees. The trail curves around the side of a steep hill, and Manitou Springs High School comes into view. The trail makes a sharp right, heading down toward the parking area. Skirt the parking area and climb on a narrow trail to the east. Look to the north for great views of the Garden of the Gods.

The trail then heads south and drops down to the Crystal Park Cemetery and the end of the route. Turn around and retrace your steps back to the trailhead.

Manitou Springs is a wonderful place to visit and enjoy. There are many interesting shops, along with a number of excellent restaurants, coffee shops, and bars. The town is very walker friendly, and exploring the side streets is a great way to spend some time after your hike.

Miles and Directions

0.0 Start from the parking area and head south on the marked Paul Intemann Trail.

0.1 Pass an old service road.

0.2 Pass through a gate.

0.4 Arrive at a bench and overlook.

0.6 Junction with the Red Mountain Trail.

1.1 Cross over Delaware Avenue.

1.4 Pass through old stone pillars.

1.7 Arrive at a small playground.

2.7 Crystal Park Cemetery. Retrace your steps.

5.4 Arrive back at the trailhead.

60 Waldo Canyon

This beautiful hike up into Waldo Canyon, with spectacular views of Colorado Springs, Pikes Peak, and Ute Pass, is extremely popular on the weekends. Plan on doing your hike midweek or in the early morning.

Start: From the parking area, climb up a series of steep steps to the start of the Waldo Canyon Trail.
Distance: 7.0-mile loop
Hiking time: About 2.5 to 3.5 hours
Difficulty: Moderate
Trail surface: Can be rocky
Seasons: Year-round

Other trail users: Mountain bikers
Canine compatibility: Dogs must be on leash
Maps: Trails Illustrated Pikes Peak/Canon City #135
Trail contact: Pike National Forest; (719) 636-1602; www.gorp.com/parks-guide/travel-ta-pike-national-forest-hiking-colorado-sidwcmdev_066073.html#ixzz1jw1diSgJ

Finding the trailhead: From Colorado Springs, take US 24 west, up Ute Pass, to Waldo Canyon. The parking area is on the right, 3.5 miles past Manitou Springs. GPS: N38 52.5338' / W104 56.5835'

The Hike

From the parking area, climb up a series of steep steps to the start of the Waldo Canyon Trail. The trail becomes level and heads to the east, past a registration box, to an overlook on the right. Beyond the overlook and interpretive sign the trail heads north, and contours around the side of a steep hill. Views open to the east of Colorado Springs, and up and down Fountain Creek Canyon and US 24.

The trail is wide and travels through an area of junipers, pinyon pines, Gambel oak, yuccas, mahogany oak, and cacti. The south-facing slope receives a lot of sun, and wildflowers thrive in the early summer months in the barren-looking, rocky soil.

At around the 1-mile mark the trail gains a ridge and makes a left into Waldo Canyon. The trail drops for a short distance, past several rocky sections. The narrow path then cuts across a steep slope through a dense forest of Douglas firs. Enjoying the

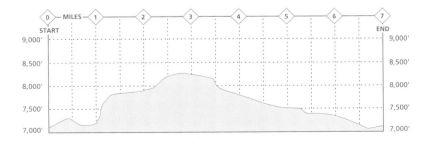

Hikers enjoying this popular trail

shade of the tall trees, drop down into an open meadow, past several campfire rings and campsites on the right.

Reach a trail sign and small seasonal stream, and the start of the Waldo Canyon upper loop. Take a short break and soak your feet in the cool waters of the stream. If you have the kids along and they are tired, this might be a good spot to turn around and head back to the parking area.

After a short rest, take the left fork and follow the trail deep into Waldo Canyon, with the stream on the right. The trail is rocky and filled with roots. Ponderosas, Douglas firs, and blue spruce grow here, along with the occasional aspen and cotton-wood. Water-loving wildflowers grow along the moist stream and are quite colorful during the summer months.

The trail climbs at a steady rate and soon reaches a series of steep steps and a trail junction. The left trail heads west toward Cascade. Stay right on the Waldo Canyon Trail, and climb through a rocky section, gaining a ridge and the high point of the hike at 8,000 feet (around the 3-mile mark). There are spectacular views south to the towering summit of Pikes Peak (14,110 feet) and down Waldo Canyon.

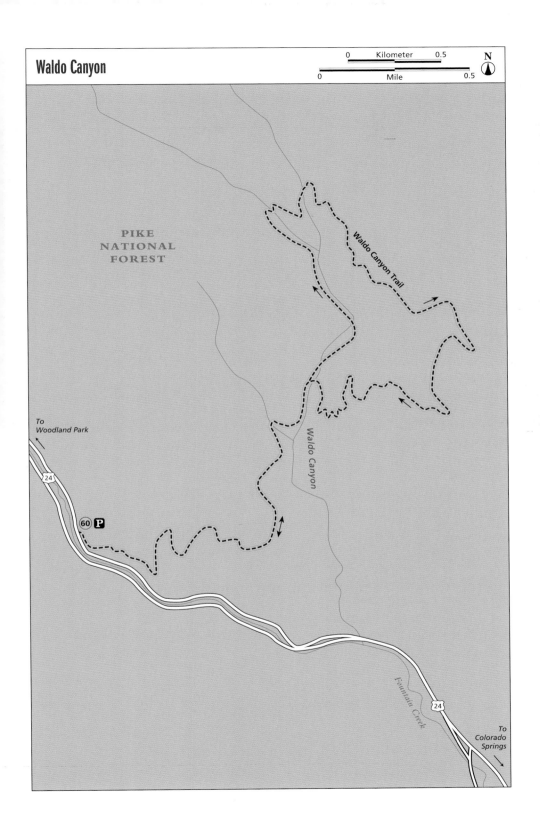

Great views looking west up Ute Pass

The trail contours back to the east and south along a ridgeline. Leaving the ridge, you begin a nice descent back into Waldo Canyon, curving back to the south, with open views of Pikes Peak, Cheyenne Mountain, Colorado Springs, and the plains. At around the 4.9-mile mark, you'll reach a series of steep switchbacks that drop you quickly back to the stream, the trail sign, and the end of the upper loop.

Retrace your route, climbing gently out of Waldo Canyon, with views of the limestone cliffs of Williams Canyon and Pikes Peak, then back to the trailhead.

Miles and Directions

0.0 Start by climbing steps to the Waldo Canyon Trail.

0.1 Overlook and interpretive sign.

0.8 Ridge and view of Williams Canyon.

1.7 Sign and start of upper loop.

2.5 Stairs and trail junction.

4.9 Switchbacks.

5.3 Back at the sign.

7.0 Arrive back at the trailhead.

Appendix A

Resources

Barr Lake State Park
13410 Picadilly Rd.
Brighton, CO 80603
(303) 659-6005

Boulder Chamber of Commerce
2440 Pearl St.
Boulder, CO 80302
(303) 442-1044

Boulder Ranger District
2140 Yarmouth Ave.
Boulder, CO 80301
(303) 444-6600

Canyon Lakes Ranger District
1311 South College
Fort Collins, CO 80452
(970) 498-2770

City of Boulder Open Space
1300 Canyon Blvd.
Boulder, CO 80302
(303) 441-3400

Clear Creek Ranger District
101 Chicago Creek/PO Box 3307
Idaho Springs, CO 80452
(303) 567-3000

Colorado Springs Convention &
Visitors Bureau
515 South Cascade
Colorado Springs, CO 80903
(719) 635-7506 or (800) DO-VISIT

Colorado State Parks
1313 Sherman St., #618
Denver, CO 80203
(303) 866-3437

Denver Metro Convention &
Visitors Bureau
1555 California St.
Denver, CO 80202
(303) 892-1112

Eldorado Canyon State Park
PO Box B
Eldorado Springs, CO 80025
(303) 494-3943

Fort Collins Convention &
Visitors Bureau
420 S. Howes St., Suite 101/PO Box
1998
Fort Collins, CO 80522
(970) 482-5821

Golden Gate State Park
3873 CO 46
Golden, CO 80403
(303) 583-3707

Horsetooth Mountain and
Reservoir Parks
Larimer County Parks Department
1800 South CR 31
Loveland, CO 80537
(970) 226-4517

Jefferson County Open Space
700 Jefferson County Pkwy., Suite 100
Golden, CO 80401
(303) 271-5925

Lory State Park
708 Lodgepole Dr.
Bellevue, CO 80512
(970) 493-1623

Rocky Mountain National Park
1000 US 36
Estes Park, CO 80517
(970) 586-1206

South Platte District
19316 Goddard Ranch Ct.
Morrison, CO 80465
(303) 697-0414

Sulfur Ranger District
9 Ten Mile Dr./PO Box 10
Granby, CO 80446
(970) 887-4100

Appendix B

The Hiker's Checklist

Always make and check your own checklist!

If you've ever hiked into the backcountry and discovered that you've forgotten an essential, you know that it's a good idea to make a checklist and check the items off as you pack so that you won't forget the things you want and need. Here are some ideas:

Clothing

- ❏ Dependable rain parka
- ❏ Rain pants
- ❏ Windbreaker
- ❏ Thermal underwear
- ❏ Shorts
- ❏ Long pants or sweatpants
- ❏ Wool cap or balaclava
- ❏ Hat
- ❏ Wool shirt or sweater
- ❏ Jacket or parka
- ❏ Extra socks
- ❏ Underwear
- ❏ Lightweight shirts
- ❏ T-shirts
- ❏ Bandanna(s)
- ❏ Mittens or gloves
- ❏ Belt

Footwear

- ❏ Sturdy, comfortable boots
- ❏ Lightweight camp shoes

Bedding

- ❏ Sleeping bag
- ❏ Foam pad or air mattress
- ❏ Groundsheet (plastic or nylon)
- ❏ Dependable tent

Hauling

- ❏ Backpack and/or day pack

Cooking

- ❏ 1-quart container (plastic)
- ❏ 1-gallon water container for camp use (collapsible)
- ❏ Backpack stove and extra fuel
- ❏ Funnel
- ❏ Aluminum foil
- ❏ Cooking pots
- ❏ Bowls/plates
- ❏ Utensils (spoons, forks, small spatula, knife)
- ❏ Pot scrubber
- ❏ Matches in waterproof container

Food and drink

- ❏ Cereal
- ❏ Bread
- ❏ Crackers
- ❏ Cheese
- ❏ Trail mix
- ❏ Margarine
- ❏ Powdered soups
- ❏ Salt/pepper
- ❏ Main course meals
- ❏ Snacks
- ❏ Hot chocolate
- ❏ Tea
- ❏ Powdered milk
- ❏ Drink mixes

Photography

- ❏ Camera and film
- ❏ Filters
- ❏ Lens brush/paper

Miscellaneous

- ❑ Sunglasses
- ❑ Map and compass
- ❑ Toilet paper
- ❑ Pocketknife
- ❑ Sunscreen
- ❑ Good insect repellent
- ❑ Lip balm
- ❑ Flashlight with good batteries and a spare bulb
- ❑ Candle(s)
- ❑ First-aid kit
- ❑ Your FalconGuide
- ❑ Survival kit
- ❑ Small garden trowel or shovel
- ❑ Water filter or purification tablets
- ❑ Plastic bags (for trash)
- ❑ Soap
- ❑ Towel
- ❑ Toothbrush
- ❑ Fishing license
- ❑ Fishing rod, reel, lures, flies, etc.
- ❑ Binoculars
- ❑ Waterproof covering for pack
- ❑ Watch
- ❑ Sewing kit

About the Author

Bob D'Antonio has spent many hours hiking, biking, and climbing throughout the United States. He has written several FalconGuides on mountain biking and rock climbing, and is the author of *Hiking Colorado's Indian Peaks*. A native of Philadelphia, Pennsylvania, Bob lives in Taos, New Mexico, with his wife, Laurel, and their labrador Eva.

Your next adventure begins here.

falcon.com

American Hiking Society

Because you hike.
We're with you every step of the way

As a national voice for hikers, **American Hiking Society** works every day:

- Building and maintaining hiking trails
- Educating and supporting hikers by providing information and resources
- Supporting hiking and trail organizations nationwide
- Speaking for hikers in the halls of Congress and with federal land managers

Whether you're a casual hiker or a seasoned backpacker, become a member of American Hiking Society and join the national hiking community! You'll enjoy great member benefits and help preserve the nation's hiking trails, so tomorrow's hike is even better than today's. We invite you to join us now!

American Hiking Society

www.AmericanHiking.org • info@AmericanHiking.org